HOW TO READ A FINANCIAL REPORT

HOW TO READ A

WRINGING VITAL SIGNS OUT OF

Ninth Edition

WILEY

FINANCIAL REPORT

THE NUMBERS

JOHN A. TRACY AND **TAGE C. TRACY**

Cover Design: Wiley
Cover Illustration: Wiley

Published by John Wiley & Sons, Inc., Hoboken, New Jersey.

The Eighth Edition of How to Read a Financial Report: Wringing Vital Signs Out of the Numbers was published by John Wiley & Sons, Inc, in 2014.

Published simultaneously in Canada.

For general information on our other products and services or for technical support, please contact our Customer Care Department within the United States at (800) 762-2974, outside the United States at (317) 572-3993 or fax (317) 572-4002.

Wiley publishes in a variety of print and electronic formats and by print-on-demand. Some material included with standard print versions of this book may not be included in e-books or in print-on-demand. If this book refers to media such as a CD or DVD that is not included in the version you purchased, you may download this material at http://booksupport.wiley.com. For more information about Wiley products, visit www.wiley.com.

Library of Congress Cataloging-in-Publication Data:

Names: Tracy, John A., author. | Tracy, Tage C., author.
Title: How to read a financial report: wringing vital signs out of the
  numbers / John A. Tracy and Tage C. Tracy.
Description: Ninth edition. | Hoboken, New Jersey : Wiley, [2020] |
  Includes index.
Identifiers: LCCN 2019035972 (print) | LCCN 2019035973 (ebook) | ISBN
  9781119606468 (paperback) | ISBN 9781119606451 (Adobe PDF) | ISBN
  9781119606482 (epub)
Subjects: LCSH: Financial statements.
Classification: LCC HF5681.B2 T733 2020 (print) | LCC HF5681.B2 (ebook) |
  DDC 657/.3—dc23
LC record available at https://lccn.loc.gov/2019035972
LC ebook record available at https://lccn.loc.gov/2019035973

Printed in the United States of America.

V10016414_121919

CONTENTS

LIST OF EXHIBITS

PREFACE TO THE NINTH EDITION

This book has stood the test of time and reminds all of us that fortifying your understanding of financial reports and statements has been, is, and will always be essential evergreen knowledge. After 40 years in print, spanning nine editions, it has survived countless economic and financial challenges—and is still going strong. My son Tage joined me as coauthor in the previous edition, and I willingly share credit with him for the book's continued success.

This edition catches up with major changes in financial reporting since the eighth edition was released in 2013. It also expands our discussion on how financial results are communicated. At the same time, however, the architecture of the book remains unchanged. The framework of the book has proved very successful for 40 years so I'd be a fool to mess with this winning formula. (My mother did not raise a fool.)

Cash flows are underscored throughout the book and remain a central focus of the current edition. In business, everything starts and ends with cash flow, which is a concept we never stray too far from.

As with all previous editions, our book explains the connectivity of the different pieces of information reported in financial statements. In reading financial statements you need to know how the different elements are connected. You cannot grab one piece of information in one place and ignore its other dimensions and contexts. Financial statements are, essentially, spreadsheets, although they do not demonstrate what's connected to what.

We have prepared all the exhibits in the book as Excel worksheets. To request a copy of the workbook file of all the exhibits, please feel free to contact one of us via email (me at tracyj@colorado.edu or Tage at tagetracy@cox.net).

In summary, I express my sincere thanks to all of you who have sent compliments about our book. The royalties from sales of the book are nice, but the messages from readers form the real icing on the cake.

Not many books of this ilk make it to the ninth edition. It takes a good working partnership between the author and the publisher. I most sincerely thank the many people at John Wiley & Sons who have worked with me over four decades.

Gordon B. Laing was my original editor and sponsor of the book. His superb editing was a blessing. I couldn't have done it without him.

JOHN A. TRACY

Boulder, Colorado
August 2019

Part One

FUNDAMENTALS

1

STARTING WITH CASH FLOWS

Summary of Cash Flows for a Business

Savvy business managers, lenders, and investors pay a lot of attention to *cash flows*. Cash inflows and outflows are the pulse of every business. Without a steady heartbeat of cash flows, a business would soon have to go on life support—or die. So, we start with cash flows.

Cash inflows and outflows appear in a summary of cash flows. For our example in Exhibit 1.1, we use a business that has been operating for many years. This established business makes profit regularly and, equally important, it keeps in good financial condition. It has a good credit history and banks lend money to the business on competitive terms. Its present stockholders would be willing to invest additional capital in the business, if needed. None of this comes easy. It takes good management to make profit consistently, to secure capital, and to stay out of financial trouble. Many businesses fail these imperatives, especially when the going gets tough.

Exhibit 1.1 summarizes the company's cash inflows and outflows for the year just ended, and shows two separate groups of cash flows. First are the cash flows of its profit-making activities—cash inflows from sales and cash outflows for expenses. Second are the other cash inflows and outflows of the business—raising capital, investing capital in assets, and distributing some of its profit to shareowners.

We assume you're fairly familiar with the cash inflows and outflows listed in Exhibit 1.1. Therefore, we are brief in describing the cash flows at this early point in the book:

♦ The business received $51,680,000 during the year from selling products to its customers. It should be no surprise that this is its largest source of cash inflow. Cash inflow from sales revenue is needed for paying expenses. During the year the company paid $34,760,000 for the products it sells to customers. And, it had sizable cash outflows for operating expenses, interest on its debt (borrowed money), and income tax. The net result of its cash flows of profit-making activities is a $3,105,000 cash increase for the year—an extremely important number that managers, lenders, and investors watch closely.

♦ Moving on to the second group of cash flows during the year, the business increased the amount borrowed on notes payable by $625,000 and its stockholders invested an additional $175,000 in the business. Together these two external sources of capital provided $800,000, which is in addition to the internal $3,105,000 cash from its profit-making activities during the year. On the other side of the ledger, the business spent $3,625,000 for building improvements, new machines and equipment, and intangible assets. Finally, the business distributed to its stockholders $750,000 cash from profit. This distribution from profit is included in the second group of cash flows, indicating that the $3,105,000 cash flow from profit is the net cash flow *before* the distribution to stockholders.

EXHIBIT 1.1—SUMMARY OF CASH FLOWS DURING YEAR
Dollar Amounts in Thousands

Cash Flows of Profit-Making Activities	
From sales of products to customers, which includes some sales made last year	$ 51,680
For acquiring products that were sold, or are still being held for future sale	$(34,760)
For operating expenses, some of which were incurred last year	$(11,630)
For interest on short-term and long-term debt, some of which applies to last year	$ (520)
For income tax, some of which was paid on last year's taxable income	$ (1,665)
Net cash flow from profit-making activities during year	$ 3,105
Other Sources and Uses of Cash	
From increasing amount borrowed on interest-bearing notes payable	$ 625
From issuing additional capital stock (ownership shares) in the business	$ 175
For building improvements, new machines, new equipment, and intangible assets	$ (3,625)
For distributions to stockholders from profit	$ (750)
Net cash decrease from other sources and uses	$ (3,575)
Net cash increase (decrease) during year	$ (470)

- The net result of all cash inflows and outflows is a $470,000 cash *decrease* during the year. When you see a decrease, don't jump to any conclusions. In and of itself, the net decrease in cash is neither good nor bad. You need more information than appears on the summary of cash flows to come to any conclusions about the financial performance and situation of the business.

What Does Cash Flows Summary *Not* Tell You?

In Exhibit 1.1 we see that cash, the all-important lubricant of business activity, decreased $470,000 during the period (in this case, a year). In other words, the total of cash outflows exceeded the total of cash inflows by this amount for the period. The cash decrease and the reasons for it are important information. The summary of cash flows tells us part of the story, but cash flows alone do not tell the whole story. A business's managers, investors, lenders, and other stakeholders need to know two additional pieces of information that are *not* reported in an organization's summary of cash flows. They are:

1. The *profit* earned (or *loss* suffered) by the business for the period.

2. The *financial condition* of the business at the end of the period.

Now, hold on. Exhibit 1.1 just informed us that the net cash increase from sales revenue less expenses was $3,105,000 for the year. This may lead you to ask, "Doesn't this cash increase equal the amount of profit earned for the year?" No, it doesn't. The net cash flow from profit-making operations during the period does not equal the amount of profit earned for the period. In fact, it's not unusual for these two numbers to be very different.

Profit is an *accounting-determined* number that requires much more than simply keeping track of cash flows. The differences between using a checkbook to measure profit and using accounting methods to measure profit are important to understand. Cash flows during a period are *hardly ever* the correct amounts for measuring a company's sales revenue and expenses for that period. To summarize: Profit cannot be determined from cash flows.

Furthermore, a summary of cash flows reveals virtually nothing about the *financial condition* of the business. Financial condition refers to the assets of the business matched against its liabilities at the end of the period. For example: How much cash does the company have in its checking account(s) at the end of the year? From the summary of cash flows (Exhibit 1.1) we can see that the business decreased its cash balance $470,000 during the year, but we cannot determine the company's ending cash balance. More importantly, the cash flows summary does not report the amounts of assets and liabilities of the business at the end of the period.

Profit Is Not Measured by Cash Flows

The company in this example sells products on *credit*. The business offers its customers a short period of time to pay for their purchases. Most of the company's sales are to other businesses, which demand credit. (In contrast, most retailers selling to individuals accept credit cards instead of extending credit to their customers.) In this example the company collected $51,680,000 from its customers during the year. However, some of this cash inflow was for sales made in the *previous* year. And, some sales made on credit in the year just ended had not been collected by the end of the year.

At year-end the company had *receivables* from sales made to its customers during the latter part of the year. These receivables will be collected early next year. Because some cash was collected from last year's sales and some cash was not collected from sales made in the year just ended, the total amount of cash collections during the year differs from the amount of *sales revenue* for the year.

Cash disbursements during the year are *not* the correct amounts for measuring expenses. The company paid $34,760,000 for products that could be sold to customers. At year-end, however, many products were still being held in *inventory*. These products had not yet been sold by year-end. Only the cost of products sold and delivered to customers during the year should be deducted as expense from sales revenue to measure profit. Don't you agree?

Furthermore, some of the company's product costs had not yet been paid by the end of the year. The company buys on credit and takes several weeks to pay its bills. The company has *liabilities* at year-end for recent product purchases and for operating costs. Further complicating the situation, the company makes cash payments during the year for operating expenses and interest and income tax expenses, but these are not the correct amounts for measuring profit for the year. The company has liabilities at the end of the year for unpaid expenses. The cash outflow amounts shown in Exhibit 1.1 do not include the amounts of *unpaid expenses* at the end of the year.

In short, cash flows from sales revenue and for expenses are not necessarily the correct amounts for measuring profit for a period of time. Many types of cash flows take place too late or too early so they cannot be used to correctly measure profit for a period. Correct timing is needed to record sales revenue and expenses in the right period. The amounts of cash flows caused by sales and expenses could turn out to be fairly close to the correct accounting amounts—or, they could be vastly different. Even small differences between the cash flow amounts and the correct accounting amounts can cause problems.

Cash Flows Do Not Reveal Financial Condition

The cash flows summary for the year does not reveal the financial condition of the company. Managers certainly need to know which assets the business owns and the amounts of each asset, which can include cash, receivables, inventory, among others. Also, they need to know which liabilities the company owes and the amounts of each.

Business managers have the responsibility for keeping the company in a position to pay its liabilities when they come due. In other words, managers have to keep the business *solvent* (able to pay its liabilities on time) and *liquid* (having enough available cash to meet its needs). Furthermore, managers have to know whether assets are too large (or too small) relative to the sales volume of the business. A company's lenders and investors want to know the same things.

In brief, both the managers inside the business and the lenders and investors outside the business need a summary of a company's financial condition (its assets and liabilities). They also need a profit performance report, which summarizes the company's sales revenue, expenses, and profit for the year.

In this chapter we have explained that a cash flows summary has its limits—in particular, it does not report profit and does not present the financial condition of a business. Nevertheless, a cash flows summary is useful. In fact, a different version of what is shown in Exhibit 1.1 is one of the three primary financial statements reported by every business. But in no sense does a cash flows summary take the place of the profit performance report or the financial condition report. The next chapter introduces these two financial statements. Chapter 3 then moves on to the statement of cash flows, which is a more formal financial statement than the summary discussed in this chapter.

A Final Note Before Moving On

Over the past century (and longer) the *accounting profession* has developed. One of its main functions is to prepare and report business financial statements. A primary goal of the accounting profession has been to develop and enforce accounting and financial reporting standards that apply to all businesses. In other words, there is an authoritative "rule book" that businesses should obey in accounting for profit and in reporting profit, financial condition, and cash flows. Businesses are not free to make up their own individual accounting methods and financial reporting practices. The established rules and standards are collectively referred to as *generally accepted accounting principles* (GAAP). But things are getting more complicated these days.

Presently in the United States there are continuing developments to adopt separate rules for private companies versus public companies, and for small companies versus larger companies. Furthermore, efforts to harmonize American accounting and financial reporting standards with those of other countries keep slogging along. There has been a lot of standardization. Yet, there are several areas of accounting and financial reporting in which there are differences between countries. We say more about the changing landscape of accounting and financial reporting standards in later chapters.

2

TWO BEDROCK FINANCIAL STATEMENTS

Need for Financial Information

Business managers, lenders, and investors need to know the *financial condition* of a business. They need a report that summarizes the business entity's assets and liabilities, as well as the ownership residual of its assets in excess of liabilities. And they need to know the *profit* (or *loss*) *performance* of the business. They need information that summarizes sales revenue and expenses for the most recent period and the resulting profit or loss.

The means of communicating such financial information are *financial statements*. Accountants prepare the financial statements. They are the financial scorekeepers of the entity. Financial statements are sent regularly by a business to its managers, lenders, and investors—and, anyone else with a legitimate interest in the business for that matter. Financial condition is communicated in an accounting report called the *balance sheet*. Profit-motivated activities are presented in an accounting report called the *income statement*.

Alternative titles for the balance sheet include the *statement of financial condition* or the *statement of financial position*. An income statement may be titled as a *statement of operations* or an *earnings statement*. We stick with the names *balance sheet* and *income statement* to be consistent throughout the book. Informally, financial statements are called simply *financials*.

In almost all cases financial statements are supplemented with additional information, which is presented in *footnotes* and *supporting schedules*. One very common supporting schedule is the *statement of changes in stockholders' (owners') equity*. The broader term *financial report* refers to all this, plus any additional commentary from management, narrative explanations, graphics, and promotional content that accompany the financial statements, footnotes, and supporting schedules. Distribution of the financial reports of a private business may be restricted to its top-level managers, its shareholders, and major creditors. Federal laws require publicly owned businesses to make their financial reports publicly available.

The income statement and balance sheet for the company example introduced in Chapter 1 are presented here in Exhibits 2.1 and 2.2, respectively. The format and content of these two financial

EXHIBIT 2.1 – INCOME STATEMENT FOR YEAR
Dollar Amounts in Thousands

Sales Revenue	$ 52,000
Cost of Goods Sold Expense	(33,800)
Gross Margin	$ 18,200
Selling, General, and Administrative Expenses	(12,480)
Depreciation Expense	(785)
Earnings Before Interest and Income Tax	$ 4,935
Interest Expense	(545)
Earnings Before Income Tax	$ 4,390
Income Tax Expense	(1,748)
Net Income	$ 2,642

statements apply to manufacturers, wholesalers, and retailers—businesses that make or buy *products* that are sold to their customers. Although the financial statements of service businesses that don't sell products differ somewhat, Exhibits 2.1 and 2.2 illustrate the basic framework and content of income statements and balance sheets for all businesses.

EXHIBIT 2.2—YEAR-END BALANCE SHEETS
Dollar Amounts in Thousands

	Last Year-End	This Year-End	Change		Last Year-End	This Year-End	Change
Cash	$ 3,735	$ 3,265	$ (470)	Accounts Payable	$ 2,675	$ 3,320	$ 645
Accounts Receivable	4,680	5,000	320	Accrued Expenses Payable	1,035	1,515	480
Inventory	7,515	8,450	935	Income Tax Payable	82	165	83
Prepaid Expenses	685	960	275	Short-Term Notes Payable	3,000	3,125	125
Current Assets	$ 16,615	$ 17,675		**Current Liabilities**	$ 6,792	$ 8,125	
Property, Plant, and Equipment	$ 13,450	$ 16,500	3,050	**Long-Term Notes Payable**	$ 3,750	$ 4,250	500
Accumulated Depreciation	(3,465)	(4,250)	(785)				
Cost Less Depreciation	$ 9,985	$ 12,250		Capital Stock—793,000 shares and 800,000 shares respectively	$ 7,950	$ 8,125	175
Intangible Assets	$ 5,000	$ 5,575	575	Retained Earnings	13,108	15,000	1,892
Long-Term Operating Assets	$ 14,985	$ 17,825		**Stockholders' Equity**	$ 21,058	$ 23,125	
Total Assets	$ 31,600	$ 35,500	$ 3,900	**Total Liabilities and Stockholders' Equity**	$ 31,600	$ 35,500	$ 3,900

Reporting Profit Performance: The Income Statement

The first question on everyone's mind is usually whether a business made a profit or suffered a loss and how much. Also, people are interested in the *size* of the business, which usually refers to the annual sales revenue. The income statement summarizes sales revenue and expenses for a period of time (one year in Exhibit 2.1). All the dollar amounts reported in this financial statement are cumulative totals for the whole period.

The top line identifies the total amount of proceeds or gross income from sales to customers, and is generally called *sales revenue*. The bottom line reflects *net income* (also sometimes called *net earnings*, but seldom *profit* or *net profit*). Net income is the final profit after all expenses are deducted from sales revenue. The business in this example earned $2,642,000 net income on its sales revenue of $52,000,000 for the year. In other words, after deducting all expenses, only a smidgeon more than 5 percent of the company's sales revenue remained as final profit (net income).

The income statement is read in a step-down manner, like walking down stairs. Each step down is a deduction of one or more expenses. The first step deducts the cost of goods (products) sold from the sales revenue of goods sold, which gives *gross margin*. (Note that *gross margin* is also called *gross profit*, which is one of the few terms on an income statement that contains the word *profit*.) This measure of profit is called *gross* because many other expenses have not yet been deducted.

Next, two additional expense deductions are made. The first is *selling*, *general*, and *administrative expenses*, which is a broad category of operating expenses. The second is the depreciation expense (a unique expense). Both of these are deducted from gross margin, giving *earnings before interest and income tax*. This measure of profit is also called *operating earnings* (which sometimes goes by a slightly different name). Next, interest expense on debt is deducted, which gives earnings before income tax. The last step is to deduct income tax expense, which gives net income, which appears on the bottom line on the income statement. Undoubtedly, you've heard the term "bottom line," and the placement of net income on the income statement is where it comes from. (However, this slang is not used in financial reports.)

As an aside, note that you may hear the income statement called a *profit and loss* or *P&L statement*. This title is not used in external financial reports released outside the business.

Exhibit 2.1 depicts a multiple-step income statement, which shows three intermediate measures of profit. Exhibit 2.3 depicts a single-step income statement. The single-step format reports only the final line of net income instead of calculating it various times along the way.

Publicly owned business corporations are required to report *earnings per share* (EPS), which is basically the annual net income divided by the number of capital stock shares. Privately owned

EXHIBIT 2.3   SINGLE-STEP INCOME STATEMENT

Dollar Amounts in Thousands

Sales Revenue	$ 52,000
Cost of Goods Sold Expense	$ (33,800)
Selling, General, and Administrative Expenses	$ (12,480)
Depreciation Expense	$ (785)
Interest Expense	$ (545)
Income Tax Expense	$ (1,748)
Net Income	$ 2,642

businesses don't have to report EPS, but this figure may be useful to their stockholders. We explain earnings per share in Chapter 13.

In our income statement example (Exhibit 2.1) you see five different expenses. You may find more expense lines in an income statement, but there would seldom be more than 10 or so, as a general rule. (There can be exceptions if a business has a very unusual year.) One expense that companies are required to report is cost of goods sold. Depreciation, another expense, is so unique that we prefer to report it on a separate line, but some companies do not do this. However, depreciation can be included in another operating expense in the income statement instead of being reported separately.

Other than depreciation, Exhibit 2.1 includes just one broad, all-inclusive operating expenses line, "Selling, General, and Administrative Expenses." A business has the option of disclosing two or more operating expenses, and many do. Marketing, promotional, and selling expenses often are separated from general and administration expenses. The level of detail for expenses in income statements is flexible; financial reporting standards are somewhat loose on this point.

The sales revenue and expenses reported in income statements follow generally accepted conventions, which we briefly summarize here:

- *Sales revenue:* The total amount received or to be received from the sales of products (and/or services) to customers during the period. Sales revenue is *net*, which means that discounts off list prices, prompt payment discounts, sales returns, and any other deductions from original sales prices are deducted to determine the sales revenue amount for the period. Sales taxes are not included in sales revenue, nor are excise taxes that might apply. In short, sales revenue is the amount the business should receive to cover its expenses and to provide profit (bottom-line net income).

- *Cost of goods sold expense:* The total cost of goods (products) sold to customers during the period. This is clear enough. What might not be so clear, however, is the expense of goods that were shoplifted or are otherwise missing, and write-downs due to damage and obsolescence. The cost of such *inventory shrinkage* may be included in cost of goods sold expense for the year (or, this cost may be put in another expense account instead).

- *Selling, general, and administrative expenses (operating expenses):* Broadly speaking, every expense other than cost of goods sold, interest, and income tax. This broad category is a catchall for every expense not reported separately. In our example, depreciation is broken out as a separate expense instead of being included with other operating expenses. Some companies report advertising and marketing costs separately from administrative and general costs, and some report research and development expenses separately. There are hundreds, even thousands, of specific operating expenses, some rather large and some very small. They range from salaries and wages of employees (large) to legal fees (small, one hopes).

- **Depreciation expense:** The portions of original costs of long-term assets including buildings, machinery, equipment, tools, furniture, computers, and vehicles that is recorded to expense in one period. Depreciation is the "charge" for using these so-called *fixed assets* during the period. This expense amount is not a cash outlay in the period recorded, which makes it a unique expense compared with other operating expenses.

- **Interest expense:** The amount of interest on debt (interest-bearing liabilities) for the period. Other types of financing charges may also be included, such as loan origination fees.

- **Income tax expense:** The total amount due to the government (both federal and state) on the amount of taxable income of the business during the period. Taxable income is multiplied by the appropriate tax rates. The income tax expense does not include other types of taxes, such as unemployment and Social Security taxes on the company's payroll. These other, non-income taxes are included in operating expenses.

A business may present a two- or three-year comparative income statement in its financial report. Indeed, public corporations are required to provide historical information. We need only one year to explain the income statement.

Reporting Financial Condition: The Balance Sheet

The balance sheet shown in Exhibit 2.2 follows the standardized format regarding the classification and ordering of assets, liabilities, and ownership interests in the business. Financial institutions, public utilities, railroads, and other specialized businesses use somewhat different balance sheet layouts. However, manufacturers and retailers, as well as the large majority of various types of businesses, follow the format presented in Exhibit 2.2.

The left side of the balance sheet lists *assets*. The right side of the balance sheet first lists the *liabilities* of the business, which have a higher-order claim on the assets. The sources of ownership (equity) capital in the business are presented below the liabilities. This is to emphasize that the owners or equity holders in a business (the stockholders of a business corporation) have a secondary and lower-order claim on the assets—after its liabilities are satisfied.

Roughly speaking, a balance sheet lists assets in their order of *nearness to cash*. Cash is listed first at the top of the assets. Next, receivables that will be collected in the short run are listed, and so on down the line. (In later chapters, we say much more about the cash characteristics of different assets.) Liabilities are presented in the sequence of their nearness to payment. (We discuss this point as we go along in later chapters.)

Each separate asset, liability, and stockholders' equity reported in a balance sheet is called an *account*. Every account has a name (title) and a dollar amount, which is called its *balance*. For instance, from Exhibit 2.2 at the end of the most recent year we can determine:

Name of Account	*Amount (Balance) of Account*
Inventory	$8,450,000

The other dollar amounts in the balance sheet are either subtotals or totals of account balances. For example, the $17,675,000 amount for "Current Assets" at the end of this year does not represent a single account but rather the subtotal of the four accounts making up this group of accounts. A line is drawn above a subtotal or total, indicating account balances are being added.

A double underline (such as for "Total Assets") indicates the last amount in a column. Notice also the double underline below "Net Income" in the income statement (Exhibit 2.1), indicating it is the last number in the column.

A balance sheet is prepared at the close of business on the last day of the income statement period. For example, if the income statement is for the year ending June 30, 2020, the balance sheet is prepared at midnight June 30, 2020. The amounts reported in the balance sheet are the balances of the accounts at that precise moment in time. The financial condition of the business is frozen for one split second. A business should be careful to make a precise and accurate cutoff to separate transactions between the period just ended and next period.

A balance sheet does not report the flows of activities in the company's assets, liabilities, and shareowners' equity accounts during the period. Only the ending balances at the moment the balance sheet is prepared are reported for the accounts. For example, the company reports an ending cash balance of $3,265,000 at the end of its most recent year (see again Exhibit 2.2). Can you tell the total cash inflows and outflows for the year? No, not from the balance sheet; you can't even get a clue from the balance sheet alone.

A balance sheet can be presented in the landscape (horizontal) layout mode as shown in Exhibit 2.2, or in the portrait (vertical) layout. The accounts reported in the balance sheet are not thrown together haphazardly in no particular order. According to long-standing rules, balance sheet accounts are subdivided into the following classes, or basic groups, in the following order of presentation:

Left Side (or Top Section)	Right Side (or Bottom Section)
Current assets	Current liabilities
Long-term operating assets	Long-term liabilities
Other assets	Owners' equity

Current assets are cash and other assets that will be converted into cash during one *operating cycle*. The operating cycle refers to the sequence of buying or manufacturing products, holding the products until sale, selling the products, waiting to collect the receivables from the sales, and finally receiving cash from customers. This sequence is the most basic rhythm of a company's operations; it is repeated over and over. The operating cycle may be short, 60 days or less, or it may be relatively long, taking 180 days or more.

Assets not directly required in the operating cycle, such as marketable securities held as temporary investments or short-term loans made to employees, are included in the current assets class if they will be converted into cash during the coming year. A business pays in advance for some costs of operations that will not be charged to expense until next period. These *prepaid* expenses are included in current assets, as you see in Exhibit 2.2.

The second group of assets is labeled "Long-Term Operating Assets" in the balance sheet. These assets are not held for sale to customers; rather, they are used in the operations of the business. Broadly speaking, these assets fall into two groups: *tangible* and *intangible* assets. Tangible assets have physical existence, such as machines and buildings. Intangible assets do not have physical existence, but they are legally protected rights (such as patents and trademarks), or they are such things as secret processes and well-known favorable reputations that give businesses important competitive advantages. Generally intangible assets are recorded only when the assets are purchased from a source outside the business.

The tangible assets of the business are reported in the "Property, Plant, and Equipment" account (see Exhibit 2.2 again). More informally, these assets are called *fixed assets*, although this term is generally not used in balance sheets. The word *fixed* is a little strong; these assets are not really fixed or permanent, except for the land owned by a business. More accurately, these assets are the long-term operating resources used over several years—such as buildings, machinery, equipment, trucks, forklifts, furniture, computers, and telephones.

The cost of a fixed asset—with the exception of land—is gradually charged off to expense over its useful life. Each period of use thereby bears its share of the total cost of each fixed asset. This apportionment of the cost of fixed assets over their useful lives is called *depreciation*. The amount of depreciation for one year is reported as an expense in the income statement (see Exhibit 2.1). The cumulative amount that has been recorded as depreciation expense since the date of acquisition up to the balance sheet date is reported in the *accumulated depreciation* account in the balance sheet (see Exhibit 2.2). As you see, the balance in the accumulated depreciation account is deducted from the original cost of the fixed assets.

In the example, the business owns various intangible long-term operating assets. These assets report the cost of acquisition. The cost of an intangible asset remains on the books until the business determines that the asset has lost value or no longer has economic benefit. At that time the business writes down (or writes off) the original cost of the intangible asset and charges the amount to an expense, usually *amortization expense*. At one time the general practice was to allocate the cost of intangible assets over arbitrary time periods. However, many intangible assets have indefinite and indeterminable useful lives. The conventional wisdom now is that it's better to wait until an intangible asset has lost value, at which time an expense is recorded.

You may see an account called "Other Assets" on a balance sheet, which is a catchall title for assets that don't fit in the current assets or long-term operating assets classes. The company in Exhibit 2.2 does not have any such other assets.

The accounts reported in the *current liabilities* class are short-term liabilities that, for the most part, depend on the conversion of current assets into cash for their payment. Also, debts (borrowed money) that will come due within one year from the balance sheet date are put in this group. In our example, there are four accounts in current liabilities. We explain these different types of current liabilities in later chapters.

Long-term liabilities, labeled "Long-Term Notes Payable" in Exhibit 2.2, are those whose maturity dates are more than one year after the balance sheet date. There's only one such account in our example. Either in the balance sheet or in a footnote, the maturity dates, interest rates, and other relevant provisions of long-term liabilities are disclosed. To simplify, we do not include footnotes with our financial statements example in this chapter. (We discuss footnotes in Chapter 16.)

Liabilities are claims on the assets of a business. Cash or other assets that will be later converted into cash will be used to pay the liabilities. (Also, cash generated by future profit earned by the business will be available to pay the business's liabilities.) Clearly, all liabilities of a business should be reported in its balance sheet to give a complete picture of the financial condition of a business.

Liabilities are also sources of assets. For example, cash increases when a business borrows money. Inventory increases when a business buys products on credit and incurs a liability that will be paid later. Also, typically a business has liabilities for unpaid expenses and has not yet used cash to pay these liabilities. Another reason for reporting liabilities in the balance sheet is to account for the sources of the company's assets, to answer the question: Where did the company's total assets come from?

Some part of the total assets of a business comes not from liabilities but from its owners investing capital in the business and from retaining some or all of the profit the business earns that is not distributed to its owners. In this example the business is organized legally as a corporation. Its *stockholders' equity* accounts in the balance sheet reveal the sources of the company's total assets in excess of its total liabilities. Notice in Exhibit 2.2 the two stockholders' (owners') equity sources, which are called *capital stock* and *retained earnings*.

When owners (stockholders of a business corporation) invest capital in the business, the capital stock account is increased. Net income earned by a business less the amount distributed to owners increases the retained earnings account. The nature of retained earnings can be confusing; therefore, we explain this account in depth at the appropriate places in the book. Just a quick word of advice here: Retained earnings is *not*—we repeat, *not*—an asset. Get such a notion out of your head.

3

REPORTING CASH FLOWS

Statement of Cash Flows

Chapter 2 introduces the two hardcore financial statements that are included in the financial report of a business, the income statement (Exhibit 2.1) and the balance sheet (Exhibit 2.2). Both of these provide a comprehensive summary of the financial performance and financial condition of the business; however, this is not the end of the story. Financial reporting standards require that a *statement of cash flows* also be presented for the same time period as the income statement.

This third financial statement, as its title implies, focuses on the cash flows of the period. The cash flow statement is not more important than the income statement and balance sheet. Rather, it discloses additional information that supplements the income statement and balance sheet.

Exhibit 3.1 presents the statement of cash flows for our business example. This financial statement has three parts, or *layers*: 1) cash flows from *operating* activities, 2) cash flows from *investing* activities, and 3) cash flows from *financing* activities. Operating activities relate to the profit-making activities of the business. Of course, a business may suffer a loss instead of making profit. On a statement of cash flows, the term "operating activities" refers to revenue and expenses (as well as gains and losses) during the period that culminate in the bottom-line net income or loss for the period.

The income statement of our business example (Exhibit 2.1) divulges 10 lines of information and its balance sheet has 21 lines. So, already you have 31 items of information, which take time to read. The statement of cash flows adds another 20 lines of information to read. Is this financial statement worth the additional time it takes to read it? What's the payoff?

EXHIBIT 3.1–STATEMENT OF CASH FLOWS FOR YEAR
Dollar Amounts in Thousands

Cash Flow from Operating Activities		
Net Income (from Income Statement)	$ 2,642	
Accounts Receivable Increase	(320)	
Inventory Increase	(935)	
Prepaid Expenses Increase	(275)	
Depreciation Expense	785	
Accounts Payable Increase	645	
Accrued Expenses Payable Increase	480	
Income Tax Payable Increase	83	$ 3,105
Cash Flow from Investing Activities		
Expenditures for Property, Plant, and Equipment	$ (3,050)	
Expenditures for Intangible Assets	(575)	(3,625)
Cash Flow from Financing Activities		
Increase in Short-Term Debt	$ 125	
Increase in Long-Term Debt	500	
Issuance of Additional Capital Stock Shares	175	
Distribution of Cash Dividends from Profit	(750)	50
Decrease in Cash During Year		$ (470)
Cash Balance at Start of Year		3,735
Cash Balance at End of Year		$ 3,265

For many financial report readers, the main value of the statement of cash flows is that it discloses the *cash flow from operating activities*. They zero in on this number, and may not read any other line of information in the financial statement. This key metric is commonly called *cash flow from profit*. In its income statement for the year (Exhibit 2.1), the company reports that it earned $2,642,000 net income, or bottom-line profit. In its statement of cash flows for the year (Exhibit 3.1) the company reports that it generated $3,105,000 cash flow from operating activities, that is, from profit-making activities. In short, profit is $2,642,000 in one financial statement and $3,105,000 in another statement. This can be confusing, to say the least.

How can cash flow from profit be higher than profit? Is one of the two numbers *fake* profit? Where did the *extra* cash come from? In other situations, could cash flow be less than profit? (Yes, it can be.) A short explanation for this discrepancy is that actual cash inflow from revenue is typically somewhat higher or lower than the amount of revenue recorded for the period. And, actual cash outflows for expenses typically differ from the amounts of expenses recorded for the period.

Cash Versus Accrual Accounting

The first section of the statement of cash flows attempts to explain the differences between cash flows and revenue and expenses, line by line. But in our experience business managers, lenders, and investors generally cannot make heads or tails of this section of the cash flows statement. The main reason is that they don't have a clear picture of how revenue and expenses are recorded. Do you?

Exhibit 3.2 compares the company's revenue and expenses cash flows for the year with its revenue and expenses amounts for the year. The amounts for revenue and expenses are recorded on the *accrual basis*. This means that the transactions and other developments that affect the business are recorded when the economic event takes place, which is often before or after when cash actually changes hands. For example, this company, like many businesses, offers its customers credit. The sale is made today, but the business does not collect cash until a month or two later. The sale is recorded today but the corresponding cash is not recorded until later.

Notice in Exhibit 3.2 that the differences between cash flows and accrual amounts do not differ too much—except for those related to *depreciation*. The cost of a long-term operating asset, such as a building or piece of heavy equipment, for example, is allocated over the operating life of the asset. The allocation of its cost over the useful life of an asset is a prime example of the accrual basis of accounting. Deprecation for the year is not a cash outlay; cash was paid when the asset was acquired. Notice in the "Investing" section of the cash flows statement that the business made major cash outlays for long-term operating assets.

A document comparing cash flows with accrual amounts, like the one shown in Exhibit 3.2, is a tool of explanation. It is not a

EXHIBIT 3.2—REVENUE AND EXPENSES: CASH FLOWS VERSUS ACCRUAL AMOUNTS

Dollar Amounts in Thousands for Year Just Ended

	Cash Flow Amounts	Accrual Amounts
Sales of Products	$ 51,680	$ 52,000
Cost of Products	$(34,760)	$(33,800)
Operating Costs	$(11,630)	$(12,480)
Depreciation Costs	$ 0	$ (785)
Interest on Debt	$ (520)	$ (545)
Income Tax	$ (1,665)	$ (1,748)
Net Amount	$ 3,105	$ 2,642

financial statement. It is not included in a financial report with the three required financial statements (i.e., income statement, balance sheet, and cash flows statement). Exhibit 3.2 should help you understand why cash flow from operating activities differs from bottom-line net income for the year. In reading an income statement, keep in mind that you are reading *accrual-based* amounts for revenue and expenses. Bottom-line net income is an accrual-based number. The net cash flow result of revenue and expenses is found in the statement of cash flows. Chapter 14 offers further analysis of cash flow, in particular cash flow from profit (or loss if that's the case).

Financial Tasks of Business Managers

So far, we have introduced the three primary financial statements for a representative business example. These statements include: its income statement for the year just ended, its balance sheet at the end of the year, and its statement of cash flows for the year. Suppose you're one of the *outside* stockholders of the business, meaning you're not involved in managing the business but you have a fair amount of money invested in the business. You just received the financial report from the business. What should you look for? Here are some things that you might study to get started.

We call your attention to stockholders' equity in the balance sheet. Its owners (one of whom is you) have invested $8,125,000 capital in the business for which it issued capital stock shares to them. (See the *capital stock* account in Exhibit 2.2.) Furthermore, over the years the business has retained $15,000,000 profit, which is called *retained earnings*. Taken together these two sources of owners' equity equal $23,125,000. One purpose of the balance sheet is to disclose such information about the ownership of the business entity and the sources of its equity capital.

The stockholders expect the managers of the business to earn a reasonable annual return on their $23,125,000 equity ownership in the business. In its most recent annual income statement the business reports $2,642,000 bottom-line profit, or net income. This profit equals 11 percent on the company's year-end stockholders' equity. The stockholders, as well as the company's managers and its lenders, want to know more than just bottom-line profit. They want to see the whole picture of how profit is earned. Therefore, the income statement reports totals for revenue and expenses for the period as well as bottom-line net income.

The ability of managers to make sales and to control expenses, and thereby earn profit, is summarized in the income statement. Business investors and lenders pay particular attention to the profit yield from revenue. Earning profit is essential for survival and it is the business manager's most important financial imperative. But the bottom line is not the end of the manager's job—not by a long shot!

To earn profit and stay out of trouble, managers must control the *financial condition* of the business. This means, among other things, keeping assets and liabilities within appropriate limits and proportions relative to each other and relative to the sales revenue and expenses of the business. Managers must prevent cash shortages that would cause the business to default on its liabilities when they come due, or not be able to meet its payroll on time.

Business managers really have a threefold financial task: 1) earning enough profit, 2) controlling the company's assets and liabilities, and 3) generating cash flows. For all businesses, regardless of size, a financial statement is prepared for each financial imperative—one for profit performance (the income statement), one for financial condition (the balance sheet), and the statement of cash flows.

Earning adequate profit by itself does not guarantee survival and good cash flow. A business manager cannot fully manage profit without also managing the assets and liabilities of sales revenue and expenses. In our business example, the changes in these assets and liabilities cause cash flow to be higher than the profit for the year. In other situations, the changes can cause cash flow from profit to be lower—perhaps much lower—than profit for the period (and can cause negative cash flow in extreme situations).

Business managers use their income statements to evaluate profit performance and to ask a raft of profit-oriented questions. Did sales revenue meet the goals and objectives for the period? Why did sales revenue increase compared with last period? Which expenses increased more or less than they should have? And there are many more such questions. These profit analysis questions are absolutely essential. But the manager can't stop at the end of these questions.

Beyond profit analysis, business managers should move on to financial condition analysis and cash flows analysis. In large business corporations, the responsibility for financial condition and cash flow is separated from profit responsibility. The chief financial officer (CFO) of the company is responsible for financial condition and cash flow. The chief executive officer (CEO) and board of directors oversee the CFO. They need to see the big picture, which includes all three financial aspects of the business—profit, financial condition, and cash flow.

In smaller businesses the president or the owner/manager is directly involved in controlling financial condition and cash flow. There's no one to delegate these responsibilities to, although, consultants and advisors can be hired for advice.

FITTING TOGETHER FINANCIAL STATEMENTS

Chapters 2 and 3 introduce the balance sheet, income statement, and statement of cash flows for a business example, as you would see these three primary financial statements in a financial report. Each statement stands alone, by itself, on a separate page in the financial report. Each statement is presented like a tub standing on its own feet. The connections between the three financial statements are not made explicit. There is no clear trail of the crossover effects between the three financial statements. But, in fact, there are dual effects—specifically, what happens in one statement also happens in another financial statement. In this chapter we explain how the financial statements interrelate.

One Problem in Financial Reporting

When preparing a financial report, accountants assume that the readers understand the interactions and mutual dependencies among the financial statements that constitute the core of the financial report. Accountants also assume that readers make use of these connections in analyzing the financial affairs of the business. Accountants assume a lot, don't they? Financial report readers can easily miss the vital interplay among the income statement, balance sheet, and statement of cash flows.

Exhibit 4.1 lays out the connections between the income statement and the balance sheet. This exhibit shows the lines of connection between sales revenue and expenses and their corresponding assets and liabilities. Exhibit 4.2 shows the connections between the changes during the year in the balance sheet accounts and the statement of cash flows. The three financial statements fit together like tongue-in-groove woodwork. The income statement, balance sheet, and cash flows statement interlock with one another.

EXHIBIT 4.1—CONNECTING ANNUAL INCOME STATEMENT WITH YEAR-END BALANCE SHEET

(Dollar Amounts in Thousands)

BALANCE SHEET	
ASSETS	

INCOME STATEMENT			BALANCE SHEET	
			ASSETS	
			Cash	$ 3,265
Sales Revenue	$ 52,000		Accounts Receivable	$ 5,000
			Inventory	$ 8,450
Cost of Goods Sold Expense	$ (33,800)		Prepaid Expenses	$ 960
Gross Margin	$ 18,200		Property, Plant, and Equipment	$ 16,500
			Accumulated Depreciation	$ (4,250)
Selling, General, and Administrative Expenses	$ (12,480)		Intangible Assets	$ 5,575
Depreciation Expense	$ (785)		**Total Assets**	$ 35,500
Operating Earnings	$ 4,935			
			LIABILITIES	
Interest Expense	$ (545)		Accounts Payable	$ 3,320
Earnings Before Income Tax	$ 4,390		Accrued Expenses Payable	$ 1,515
Income Tax Expense	$ (1,748)		Income Tax Payable	$ 165
Net Income	$ 2,642		Short-Term Notes Payable	$ 3,125
			Long-Term Notes Payable	$ 4,250
			STOCKHOLDERS' EQUITY	
			Capital Stock	$ 8,125
			Retained Earnings	$ 15,000
			Total Liabilities and Stockholders' Equity	$ 35,500

EXHIBIT 4.2—CONNECTING BALANCE SHEET CHANGES WITH STATEMENT OF CASH FLOWS

(Dollar Amounts in Thousands)

BALANCE SHEET	Changes During Year		STATEMENT OF CASH FLOWS	
ASSETS				
Cash	$ (470)		***Operating Activities***	
Accounts Receivable	$ 320		Net Income from Income Statement	$ 2,642
Inventory	$ 935		Accounts Receivable Increase	$ (320)
Prepaid Expenses	$ 275		Inventory Increase	$ (935)
			Prepaid Expenses Increase	$ (275)
Property, Plant, and Equipment	$ 3,050		Depreciation Expense	$ 785
Accumulated Depreciation	$ (785)		Accounts Payable Increase	$ 645
			Accrued Expenses Payable Increase	$ 480
Intangible Assets	$ 575		Income Tax Payable Increase	$ 83
			Cash Flow from Operating Activities	$ 3,105
Total Assets	$ 3,900			
			Investing Activities	
LIABILITIES			Expenditures for property,	
Accounts Payable	$ 645		plant, and equipment	$ (3,050)
			Expenditures for intangible assets	$ (575)
Accrued Expenses Payable	$ 480		**Cash Flow from Investing Activities**	$ (3,625)
Income Tax Payable	$ 83		***Financing Activities***	
			Short-Term Debt Increase	$ 125
Short-Term Notes Payable	$ 125		Long-Term Debt Increase	$ 500
Long-Term Notes Payable	$ 500		Issue of Additional Capital Stock Shares	$ 175
			Cash Dividends from Profit	$ (750)
STOCKHOLDERS' EQUITY			**Cash Flow from Financing Activities**	$ 50
Capital Stock	$ 175			
Retained Earnings	$ 1,892		Decrease in Cash During Year	$ (470)
			Cash Balance at Start of Year	$ 3,735
Total Liabilities and Stockholders' Equity	$ 3,900		Cash Balance at End of Year	$ 3,265

As we move along in this chapter, keep in mind that Exhibits 4.1 and 4.2 are tools of explanation. Financial reports do not include such exhibits with lines of connection. Our purpose is to show you how the financial statements in a financial report—although shown separately—are in fact interdependent. Chapters 5 through 14 explain each line of connection in the two exhibits.

Connecting the Dots

Note that in Exhibits 4.1 and 4.2 the balance sheet is presented in the *vertical*, or portrait format, also called the *report form*—assets on top, and liabilities and stockholders' equity below. To save space we do not include subtotals for current assets, current liabilities, and stockholders' equity in the balance sheet. (You might quickly compare the balance sheet in Exhibit 4.1 with the balance sheet example in Exhibit 2.2.)

In Exhibit 4.1 the lines of connection are to the *ending balances* of the assets and liabilities. In following chapters we examine how large these ending balances in assets and liabilities should be relative to the amounts of revenue and expenses for the year.

Exhibit 4.2 shows the *changes* in the balance sheet accounts during the year. These changes go to or come from the statement of cash flows. The first section of the statement uses the changes in the assets and liabilities of recording revenue and expenses to reconcile net income and *cash flow from operating activities*. This important cash flow number is the net increase or decrease in cash that is attributable to the profit-making (operating) activities of the business.

The cash increase from the company's profit-making activities for the year is $3,105,000 (see Exhibit 4.2), which compared with its $2,642,000 net income is a fairly significant difference. In this particular example, the company's cash flow from profit is $463,000 higher than its profit for the year. (In Chapter 14 we explain how the changes in assets and liabilities caused by revenue

and expenses determine the difference between cash flow and profit.)

The other, or *nonoperating*, cash flows of the business during the year are reported in the "Investing" and "Financing" sections of the statement of cash flows. See Exhibit 4.2 again. The business made key decisions during the year that required major outlays of cash, and it secured additional cash during the year from its lenders and stockholders. Notice that the lines of connection for these cash flow decisions go from the cash flow sources and uses to their respective assets, liabilities, and stockholders' equity.

You really can't swallow all the information in Exhibits 4.1 and 4.2 in one gulp. You have to drink one sip at a time. The exhibits serve as road maps that we refer to frequently in the following chapters—so that we don't lose sight of the big picture as we travel down the particular highways of connection between the financial statements.

Before moving on, we should repeat that financial statements are not presented with lines of connection as shown in Exhibits 4.1 and 4.2. You never see tether lines like this between the financial statements. As we have already mentioned above, accountants assume that the financial statement readers mentally fill in the connections that are shown in Exhibits 4.1 and 4.2. Accountants assume too much, in our opinion. It would be helpful if a financial report included reminders of the connections among the three financial statements.

In our experience, business managers and executives, and for that matter even some certified public accountants (CPAs), do not recognize the connecting links among the financial statements that we show in Exhibit 4.1. Over the years, we have corresponded with many readers who have requested the Microsoft Excel workbook file of the exhibits in this book. (See the preface for how to request this via email.) Over and over they mention one point—the value of seeing the connections among the financial statements.

Author John Tracy did not fully understand these connections himself until he started teaching at the University of California at Berkeley in 1961. In browsing through an old, out-of-print textbook, he came upon the point that financial statements, although presented separately, are articulated with one another. Even though John already had earned his PhD, he had not seen this critical point before. He was struck by the term *articulated*. In his mind's eye John could see an articulated bus, a bus having two compartments that were connected together.

Part Two

CONNECTIONS

Part Two

CONNECTIONS

5

SALES REVENUE AND ACCOUNTS RECEIVABLE

EXHIBIT 5.1 SALES REVENUE AND ACCOUNTS RECEIVABLE
Dollar Amounts in Thousands

INCOME STATEMENT FOR YEAR

Sales Revenue	$ 52,000
Cost of Goods Sold Expense	$ (33,800)
Selling, General, and Administrative Expenses	$ (12,480)
Depreciation Expense	$ (785)
Interest Expense	$ (545)
Income Tax Expense	$ (1,748)
Net Income	$ 2,642

Assuming five weeks of annual sales revenue is uncollected at year-end the ending balance of Accounts Receivable is:

5/52 × $52,000 = $5,000

BALANCE SHEET AT YEAR-END

ASSETS

Cash	$ 3,265
Accounts Receivable	$ 5,000
Inventory	$ 8,450
Prepaid Expenses	$ 960
Property, Plant, and Equipment	$16,500
Accumulated Depreciation	$ (4,250)
Intangible Assets	$ 5,575
Total Assets	**$35,500**

LIABILITIES and STOCKHOLDERS' EQUITY

Accounts Payable	$ 3,320
Accrued Expenses Payable	$ 1,515
Income Tax Payable	$ 165
Short-Term Notes Payable	$ 3,125
Long-Term Notes Payable	$ 4,250
Capital Stock	$ 8,125
Retained Earnings	$15,000
Total Liabilities and Stockholders' Equity	**$35,500**

Exploring One Link at a Time

Please refer to Exhibit 5.1, which shows the connection between *sales revenue* in the income statement and the *accounts receivable* asset account in the balance sheet. This exhibit is based on Exhibit 4.1, which ties together all the connections between the annual income statement and year-end balance sheet. This chapter is the first of many that will focus on just one connection at a time. Only one line of connection is highlighted in Exhibit 5.1—the one between sales revenue in the income statement and accounts receivable in the balance sheet.

Recall that in Exhibit 5.1 the income statement and balance sheet are stripped of subtotals. (The same is true of all exhibits in the coming chapters.) For example, the income statement is a single-step statement, meaning that it does not contain lines showing gross margin and other intermediate measures of profit. Likewise, in the balance sheet no subtotals are shown for current assets and current liabilities and for the amount of property, plant, and equipment less accumulated depreciation. Excluding subtotals gives us lean and mean financial statements to work with.

Furthermore, Exhibit 5.1 does not include the company's statement of cash flows for the year. The connections between changes in the balance sheet accounts and the cash flows statement are explained in Chapters 14 and 15. The cash flows statement would be a distraction at this point.

The central idea in this and following chapters is that the profit-making activities reported in the income statement drive or determine an asset or a liability. Assets and liabilities are reported in the balance sheet. In our example the company's sales revenue for the year just ended was $52 million. Of this total sales revenue, $5 million is in the accounts receivable asset account at the end of the year. The $5 million is the portion of annual sales that has not yet been collected at the end of the year.

In the following chapters we explore each linkage between an income statement account and its connecting account in the balance sheet.

How Sales Revenue Drives Accounts Receivable

In our business example, the company made $52,000,000 total sales during the year. This is a sizable amount, equal to an average weekly sales revenue of $1,000,000. When making a sale, the total amount of the sale (i.e., the sales price times the quantity of products sold) is recorded in the *sales revenue* account. This account accumulates all sales made during the year. On the first day of the year it starts with a zero balance; at the end of the last day of the year it has a $52,000,000 balance. In short, the balance in this account at year-end is the cumulative sum of all sales for the entire year (assuming all sales are recorded).

In the example, the business makes all its sales on credit, which means that cash is not received until sometime after the time of sale. This company sells to other businesses that demand credit. (Many retailers, such as supermarkets and gas stations, make all sales for cash, or accept credit cards that are converted into cash immediately.) The amount owed to the company from making a sale on credit is immediately recorded in the accounts receivable asset account for the amount of each sale. Sometime later, when cash is collected from customers, the cash account is increased and the accounts receivable account is decreased.

Extending credit to customers creates a cash inflow lag. The accounts receivable balance is the amount of this lag. At year-end the balance in this asset account is the amount of uncollected sales revenue. Most of the sales made on credit during the year have been converted into cash by the end of the year. Also, the accounts

receivable balance at the start of the year from credit sales made last year was collected. But, many sales made during the latter part of the year just ended have not yet been collected by the end of the year. The total amount of these uncollected sales is found in the ending balance of accounts receivable.

Some of the company's customers pay quickly to take advantage of prompt payment discounts offered by the company. (These discounts on list prices reduce sales prices but speed up cash receipts.) However, the average customer waits five weeks to pay the company and forgoes the prompt payment discount. Some customers even wait 10 weeks or more to pay the company, despite the company's efforts to encourage them to pay sooner. The company puts up with these slow payers because they generate many repeat sales.

In sum, the company has a mix of quick, regular, and slow-paying customers. Suppose that the average credit period for all customers is five weeks. (This doesn't mean that every customer takes five weeks to pay, but rather that the average time before paying is five weeks.) Therefore, on average, five weeks of annual sales are still uncollected at year-end. The relationship between annual sales revenue and the ending balance of accounts receivable can be expressed as follows:

$$\frac{5}{52} \times \frac{\$52,000,000 \text{ Sales}}{\text{Revenue for the Year}} = \frac{\$5,000,000 \text{ Accounts}}{\text{Receivable at End of Year}}$$

As you see in Exhibit 5.1, the ending balance of accounts receivable is $5,000,000; this amount equals five weeks' worth of annual sales revenue. The main point is that the average sales credit period determines the size of accounts receivable. The longer the average sales credit period, the larger the accounts receivable amount.

Let's approach this key point from another direction. Suppose we didn't know the average credit period. Nevertheless, using information from the financial statements we can determine the average credit period. The first step is to calculate the following ratio:

$$\frac{\$52,000,000 \text{ Sales Revenue}}{\$5,000,000 \text{ Accounts Receivable}} = 10.4 \text{ Times}$$

This calculation gives the *accounts receivable turnover ratio*, which is 10.4 in this example. Dividing this ratio into 52 weeks gives the average sales credit period expressed in number of weeks:

$$\frac{52 \text{ Weeks}}{10.4 \text{ Accounts Receivable Turnover Ratio}} = 5 \text{ Weeks}$$

Time is the essence of the matter. What interests the business manager, and the company's creditors and investors as well, is how long it takes on average to turn accounts receivable into cash. We think the accounts receivable turnover ratio is most meaningful when it is used to determine the number of weeks (or days, if you like) it takes a company to convert its accounts receivable into cash.

You may argue that five weeks is too long an average sales credit period for the company. This is precisely the point: What should it be? The manager in charge has to decide whether the average credit period is getting out of hand. The manager can shorten credit terms, shut off credit to slow payers, or step up collection efforts.

This isn't the place to discuss customer credit policies relative to marketing strategies and customer relations, which would take us far beyond the field of accounting. But, there is an important point to make here. Assume that, without losing any sales, the company's average sales credit period had been only four weeks, instead of five weeks.

In this alternative scenario, the company's ending accounts receivable balance would have been $1,000,000 less, or $4,000,000 (4/52 × $52,000,000 annual sales revenue = $4,000,000). The company would have collected $1,000,000 more cash during the year. With this additional cash, the company could have borrowed $1,000,000 less. At an annual 6 percent interest rate, this would have saved the business $60,000 in interest before income tax. Or the owners could have invested $1,000,000 less in the business and put their money elsewhere.

The main point is that capital has a cost. Excess accounts receivable means that excess debt or excess owners' equity capital is being used by the business. The business is not as capital efficient as it should be.

A slowdown in collecting customers' receivables or a deliberate shift in business policy allowing longer credit terms causes accounts receivable to increase. Additional capital would have to be secured, or the company would have to attempt to get by on a smaller cash balance.

If you were the business manager in this example, you should decide whether the size of accounts receivable, being five weeks of annual sales revenue, is consistent with your company's sales credit terms and your collection policies. Perhaps five weeks is too long and you need to take action. If you were a creditor or an investor in the company, you should pay attention to whether the manager is allowing the average sales credit period to get out of control. A major change in the average credit period may signal a significant change in the company's policies.

Accounting Issues

Starting in this chapter and continuing in through Chapter 13, we focus on a key connection between an income statement account and its corresponding balance sheet account. We end these chapters with a brief discussion of some of the major accounting problems pertaining to the topics discussed in the chapter.

These short discussions of accounting issues barely scratch the surface. Nevertheless, you should be aware that the numbers you see in financial statements depend on the exact accounting methods used to recognize and record those numbers. The chief accounting officer of every business must decide which accounting methods to use to record sales revenue and expenses. These accounting decisions often require tough and somewhat arbitrary choices between alternative methods.

You may not be aware that accounting decisions are not entirely obvious and clear-cut in most situations. As a matter of fact, accounting methods are quite arbitrary to one degree or another in most cases. The choice of particular accounting methods makes profit lower or higher and also makes the amounts of assets and liabilities lower or higher. Revenue is either an increase in an asset or a decrease in a liability. And, an expense is either a decrease in an asset or an increase in a liability.

Revenue accounting has become a hot issue in recent years—indeed, it may be the number one issue in financial accounting and reporting. So, what are the main issues in accounting for sales and accounts receivable? The main accounting problem in recording sales is *timing*. It's not always clear exactly when a sale is completed and all terms are final and definite. For instance, customers may have the right to return products they have purchased or to take discounts from sales prices after the point of sale. Sales prices may still be negotiable even after the point of sale. Then, there are the costs of product warranties and guarantees to consider.

The asset generated by credit sales (i.e., accounts receivable) may end up being not collectible, or not fully collectible. When should the business record the expense for uncollectible receivables (called *bad debts*)?

As you can see, there are several serious problems surrounding accounting for sales. Therefore, a business should make clear in the footnotes to its financial statements the basic accounting method it uses for recording sales revenue. We discuss footnotes in Chapter 16. Take a quick look if you like.

6

COST OF GOODS SOLD EXPENSE AND INVENTORY

EXHIBIT 6.1—COST OF GOODS SOLD EXPENSE AND INVENTORY

Dollar Amounts in Thousands

INCOME STATEMENT FOR YEAR

Sales Revenue	$ 52,000
Cost of Goods Sold Expense	$ (33,800)
Selling, General, and Administrative Expenses	$ (12,480)
Depreciation Expense	$ (785)
Interest Expense	$ (545)
Income Tax Expense	$ (1,748)
Net Income	$ 2,642

> Assuming the year-end inventory of goods awaiting sale equals 13 weeks of annual cost of goods sold the ending balance of inventory is:
>
> 13/52 × $33,800 = $8,450

BALANCE SHEET AT YEAR-END

ASSETS

Cash	$ 3,265
Accounts Receivable	$ 5,000
Inventory	$ 8,450
Prepaid Expenses	$ 960
Property, Plant, and Equipment	$ 16,500
Accumulated Depreciation	$ (4,250)
Intangible Assets	$ 5,575
Total Assets	**$ 35,500**

LIABILITIES AND STOCKHOLDERS' EQUITY

Accounts Payable	$ 3,320
Accrued Expenses Payable	$ 1,515
Income Tax Payable	$ 165
Short-Term Notes Payable	$ 3,125
Long-Term Notes Payable	$ 4,250
Capital Stock	$ 8,125
Retained Earnings	$ 15,000
Total Liabilities and Stockholders' Equity	**$ 35,500**

Please refer to Exhibit 6.1 at the start of this chapter. (Chapter 5 explains the design of this exhibit, which is also used in following chapters.) This chapter focuses on the connection between *cost of goods sold expense* in the income statement and the *inventory* asset in the balance sheet. Recall that the business in the example sells products, which are also called *goods* (in general) or *merchandise* (for retailers).

Holding Products in Inventory Until They Are Sold

Cost of goods sold expense means just that: the cost of all products sold to customers during the year. Revenue from sales is recorded in the sales revenue account, which could be called the top line of the income statement (see Exhibit 6.1). The cost of goods sold expense is reported in the income statement just below sales revenue, as you can see. Cost of goods sold expense is by far the largest expense in the company's income statement, being almost three times its selling, general, and administrative expenses for the year.

Putting cost of goods sold expense first, at the head of the expenses, is logical because it's the most direct and immediate cost of selling products. Please recall that cost of goods sold expense is deducted from sales revenue in income statements so that *gross margin* can be reported. (Exhibit 2.1 shows an income statement that reports gross margin.) On the income statement in Exhibit 6.1, however, gross margin is not shown on a separate line. Nevertheless we can't emphasize enough the importance of gross margin (also called *gross profit*), so we will explore the topic a bit more here.

The word *gross* emphasizes that only cost of goods sold expense, and *no other expenses*, have been deducted from sales revenue. Understanding gross margin is the starting point for earning an adequate net income for the period. (Remember that net income is the final, bottom-line profit.) In other words, the first step is to sell products for enough gross margin so that all other expenses can be covered and the business can also earn a profit. We discuss the company's other expenses in later chapters.

You can do the arithmetic and determine that cost of goods sold expense in our example equals 65 percent of sales revenue. Therefore, gross margin equals 35 percent of sales revenue. The business sells many different products, some for more than 35 percent gross margin and some for less. In total, for all products the business sold during the year, the average gross margin is 35 percent—which is fairly typical for a broad cross section of businesses. Gross margins more than 50 percent or less than 20 percent are unusual.

To sell products, most businesses must keep a stock of products on hand, which is called *inventory*. If a company sells products, it would be a real shock to see no inventory in its balance sheet. (It's possible, but highly unlikely.) Notice in Exhibit 6.1 that the line of connection is not between sales revenue and inventory, but between cost of goods sold expense and inventory. The inventory asset is reported at cost in the balance sheet, not at its sales value.

The inventory asset account accumulates the cost of the products purchased or manufactured. Acquisition cost stays in an inventory asset account until the products are sold to customers. At the time of sale, the cost of the products is removed from inventory and charged out to cost of goods sold expense. (Products may become nonsalable or may be stolen or damaged, in which case their cost is written down or removed from inventory and the amount is charged to cost of goods sold or some other expense, which we discuss at the end of the chapter.)

The company's inventory balance at year-end—$8,450,000 in the example—is the cost of products awaiting sale next year. The $33,800,000 deducted from sales revenue in the income statement is the cost of goods that were sold during the year. None of these products were on hand in year-end inventory.

Some of the company's products are manufactured in a short time, and some take much longer. Once the production process is finished, the products are moved into the company warehouse for storage until the goods are sold and delivered to customers. Some products are sold quickly, almost right off the end of the production line. Other products sit in the warehouse many weeks before being sold. Likewise, products bought from other companies may stay in inventory only a short time or may remain in stock two or more months before being sold. This business, like most companies, sells a mix of different products—some of which have very short holding periods and others relatively long holding periods.

In the example, the company's *average* inventory holding period for all products is 13 weeks, or three months on average. This time interval includes the production process time and the warehouse storage time. For example, a product may take three weeks to manufacture and then be held in storage 10 weeks, or vice versa. Internally, manufacturers separate *work-in-process* inventory (products still in the process of being manufactured) from *finished goods* (completed inventory ready for delivery to customers). The business does not need a work-in-process account for any products it buys from other companies in a condition ready for resale. Usually only one combined inventory account is reported in externally reported balance sheets, as shown in Exhibit 6.1. Internally, many separate inventory accounts are reported to managers.

Given that its average inventory holding period is 13 weeks, the company's inventory cost can be expressed as follows:

$$\frac{13}{52} \times \frac{\$33,800,000}{\text{Cost of Goods Sold Expense for Year}} = \frac{\$8,450,000}{\text{Inventory at End of Year}}$$

Notice in Exhibit 6.1 that the company's ending inventory balance is $8,450,000.

The main point is that the average inventory holding period determines the size of inventory relative to annual cost of goods sold expense. The longer the manufacturing and warehouse holding period is, the larger the inventory amount. Business managers prefer to operate with the lowest level of inventory possible without causing lost sales due to products being out of stock when customers want to buy them. A business invests substantial capital in inventory.

Now, suppose we didn't know the company's average inventory holding period. Using information from its financial statements, we can determine it.

The first step is to calculate the following ratio:

$$\frac{\$33,800,000 \text{ Cost of Goods Sold Expense}}{\$8,450,000 \text{ Inventory}} = 4.00 \text{ Times}$$

This gives the *inventory turnover ratio*. Dividing this ratio into 52 weeks gives the average inventory holding period expressed in number of weeks:

$$\frac{52 \text{ Weeks}}{4.00 \text{ Inventory Turnover Ratio}} = 13 \text{ Weeks}$$

Time is the essence of the matter, as with the average sales credit period extended to customers. What interests the managers, as well as the company's creditors and investors, is how long the company holds inventory before products are sold. We think the inventory turnover ratio is most meaningful when used to determine the number of weeks (or days if you prefer) that it takes before inventory is sold.

Inventory Control

Is 13 weeks too long? Should the company's average inventory holding period be shorter? These are precisely the key questions business managers, creditors, and investors should get answers to. If the holding period is longer than necessary, too much capital is being tied up in inventory. Or, the company may be cash poor because it keeps too much money in inventory and not enough in the bank.

To demonstrate this key point, suppose that with better inventory management the company could have reduced its average inventory holding period to, say, 10 weeks. This would have been a rather dramatic improvement. But modern inventory management techniques such as supply-chain management promise such improvement. If the company had reduced its average inventory holding period to just 10 weeks, its ending inventory would have been:

$$\frac{10}{52} \times \begin{matrix} \$33{,}800{,}000 \\ \text{Cost of Goods Sold} \\ \text{Expense for Year} \end{matrix} = \begin{matrix} \$6{,}500{,}000 \\ \text{Ending Inventory} \end{matrix}$$

In this scenario ending inventory would be $1,950,000 smaller ($8,450,000 versus $6,500,000). The company would have needed $1,950,000 less capital, or would have had this much more cash balance at its disposal.

Caution: With only 10 weeks' inventory, the company may be unable to make some sales because certain products might not be available for immediate delivery to customers. In other words, if overall inventory is too low, stock-outs may occur. Nothing is more frustrating, especially to the sales staff, than having willing customers but no products to deliver to them. The cost of carrying inventory has to be balanced against the profit opportunities lost by not having products on hand ready for sale.

In summary, business managers, creditors, and investors should watch that the inventory holding period is neither too long nor too short. Call this the Goldilocks test. If too long, capital is being wasted; if too short, profit opportunities are being missed. Comparisons of a company's inventory holding period with those of its competitors and with historical trends provide useful benchmarks.

Accounting Issues

Accounting for cost of goods sold expense and the cost of inventory is beset with many problems. First of all, we should mention that businesses that manufacture the products have serious problems in determining the total cost per unit of the different products they produce. Believe us, this is no walk in the park.

College and university accounting programs offer one entire course on this topic (usually called cost accounting). One main problem is the allocation of *indirect* production costs to the different products that benefit from the cost. For example, how should you allocate the cost of security guards who patrol many production departments, or the depreciation on the production plant in which hundreds of different products are manufactured?

Retailers and wholesalers (distributors) buy products in a condition ready for resale. Compared with manufacturers, resellers have a much easier time determining the cost of the products they sell—although there are a few thorny problems. In any case, once acquisition costs have been recorded (for both manufacturers and resellers), another problem rears its ugly head: Product costs fluctuate over time. Period to period, product costs move up or down.

Suppose a business has acquired two units of a product, the first for $100 and the second for $104. The business sells one unit of the product. What is the correct cost to remove from the inventory asset account and to record in cost of goods sold expense? Accountants have come up with three different ways to answer this question: $100 (first-in, first-out); $102 (average cost); and, $104 (last-in, first-out). All three methods are acceptable. Different businesses use different methods.

You might think that a business would select the method that gives it the best match with its sales revenue, to get the best measure of gross margin. Generally speaking, the best method would be the one that is most consistent with how the business sets its sales prices. But this logic does not always prevail. A business selects a cost of goods sold method for other reasons, and the method may or may not jibe with its sales pricing policies.

The inventory asset account is written down to record losses from falling sales prices, lower replacement costs, damage and spoilage, and shrinkage (shoplifting and employee theft). The losses may be recorded in the cost of goods sold expense account, or be put in another expense account. Companies do not disclose where the losses from these write-downs are recorded.

Because a business has a choice of accounting methods, it should reveal its cost of goods sold expense method in the footnotes to its financial statements. If the business uses the last-in, first-out (LIFO) method, it should disclose in the footnote the approximate current cost value of its inventory as if it had been using the first-in, first-out (FIFO) method. Other unusual events, such as a major write-down of inventory, also should be disclosed in the footnote. Unfortunately, many if not most inventory footnotes are fairly technical and difficult to understand. We discuss footnotes to financial statements in Chapter 16.

7

INVENTORY AND ACCOUNTS PAYABLE

EXHIBIT 7.1—INVENTORY AND ACCOUNTS PAYABLE
Dollar Amounts in Thousands

BALANCE SHEET AT YEAR-END

ASSETS

Cash	$ 3,265
Accounts Receivable	$ 5,000
Inventory	$ 8,450
Prepaid Expenses	$ 960
Property, Plant, and Equipment	$16,500
Accumulated Depreciation	$ (4,250)
Intangible Assets	$ 5,575
Total Assets	$35,500

> Assuming the amount payable at year-end for inventory related purchases is four weeks of the 13 weeks in inventory, the year-end balance of Accounts Payable for inventory is:
>
> $4/13 \times \$8,450 = \$2,600$

INCOME STATEMENT FOR YEAR

Sales Revenue	$ 52,000
Cost of Goods Sold Expense	$(33,800)
Selling, General, and Administrative Expenses	$(12,480)
Depreciation Expense	$ (785)
Interest Expense	$ (545)
Income Tax Expense	$ (1,748)
Net Income	$ 2,642

LIABILITIES AND STOCKHOLDERS' EQUITY

Accounts Payable	$ 2,600	
Accounts Payable	$ 720	$ 3,320
Accrued Expenses Payable		$ 1,515
Income Tax Payable		$ 165
Short-Term Notes Payable		$ 3,125
Long-Term Notes Payable		$ 4,250
Capital Stock		$ 8,125
Retained Earnings		$15,000
Total Liabilities and Stockholders' Equity		$35,500

Acquiring Inventory on the Cuff

Please refer to Exhibit 7.1. This chapter focuses on the connection between the *inventory* asset account in the balance sheet and the *accounts payable* liability in the balance sheet. Virtually every business reports accounts payable in its balance sheet, which is a short-term, non–interest-bearing liability arising from buying services, supplies, materials, and products on credit.

One main source of accounts payable is from making *inventory* purchases on credit. A second source of accounts payable is from *expenses* that are not paid immediately. Therefore, at this point we divide the total balance of the company's accounts payable liability into two parts, one for each source (refer to Exhibit 7.1 again).

Remember that in the previous two chapters we connect an income statement account with a balance sheet account. In this chapter we look at a connection between two balance sheet accounts. The linkage explained in this chapter is not about how sales revenue or an expense drives an asset, but rather how inventory drives its corresponding liability. In this chapter an asset determines a liability.

In our example the company purchases some products it sells and also manufactures other products. To begin the manufacturing process, the company purchases raw materials needed in its production process. These purchases are made on credit; the company doesn't pay for these purchases right away. Also, other production inputs are bought on credit. For example, once a month the public utility sends a bill for the gas and electricity used during the month, and the company takes several weeks before paying its utility bills. The company purchases several other manufacturing inputs on credit also. And, last but not least, the company sells products that it purchases from other manufacturers, and these are bought on credit. As you probably know, a business has to maintain its credit reputation and good standing to continue buying materials, manufacturing inputs, and products on credit.

Retailers and wholesalers (distributors) don't make the products they sell; they buy products and resell them. The products they buy are in a condition ready for resale. (Well, they may have to do some unpacking of large-size containers, but you get the point.) Unless they have a lousy reputation retailers and wholesalers buy on credit and they have accounts payable from inventory purchases. Technically speaking the company in our example is both a manufacturer of some products and a reseller of other products.

In the balance sheet shown in Exhibit 7.1, the company's $2,600,000 liability for inventory purchases on credit is presented as the first of two accounts payable amounts. The company's selling, general, and administrative expenses also generate accounts payable; the total amount of these unpaid bills ($720,000) is shown as the second accounts payable liability amount (see Exhibit 7.1 again). We discuss the second source of accounts payable in Chapter 8.

Typically, a company's inventory holding period is considerably longer than its purchase credit period. In other words, accounts payable are paid much quicker than it takes to sell inventory bought on credit. In this example, the company's average inventory holding period from the start of the production process or from the date of purchase to final sale of products averages 13 weeks (which we explain in Chapter 6). But the company has to pay its accounts payable in four weeks, on average.

Some purchases are paid for quickly, to take advantage of prompt payment discounts offered by vendors. The business takes six weeks or longer to pay many other invoices. Based on its experience and policies, a business knows the average purchase credit period for its inventory-related purchases. In this example, the business takes four weeks on average to pay such liabilities.

Therefore, the year-end balance of accounts payable for inventory-related purchases on credit can be expressed as follows:

$$\frac{4}{13} \times \frac{\$8,450,000}{\text{Inventory}} = \frac{\$2,600,000}{\text{Accounts Payable}}$$

In short, this liability equals 4/13 of the inventory balance. The business gets a free ride for the first four weeks of holding inventory because it waits this long before paying for its purchases on credit. However, the remaining nine weeks of its inventory holding period have to be financed from debt and stockholders' equity sources of capital. In other words, the business has to raise capital from borrowing sources and/or from shareholders who put money in the business on a long-term basis.

Economists are fond of saying that "there's no such thing as a free lunch." With this in mind, calling the four-week delay in paying for purchases on credit a free ride is not entirely correct. Sellers that extend credit set their prices slightly higher to compensate for the delay in receiving cash from their customers. In other words, a small but hidden interest charge is built into the cost paid by the purchasers.

Accounting Issues

Several serious accounting issues concerning inventory are discussed at the end of Chapter 6. In sharp contrast, there are relatively few accounting problems concerning the accounts payable liability. The main financial reporting issue concerns *disclosure* of relevant information about this liability.

Financial statement readers are entitled to assume that the amount reported for accounts payable is the amount that will be paid in the near future. Suppose, however, that the business is in the middle of negotiations with one or more of its accounts payable creditors regarding prices and other terms. Suppose that these disagreements involve material (significant) amounts. In this situation, the business should make a disclosure about these negotiations in the footnotes to its financial statements.

Also, financial statement readers are entitled to assume that the company's accounts payable creditors (the parties to whom it owes money) do *not* have senior or prior claims ahead of other creditors and debtholders of the business. In other words, the accounts payable creditors are assumed to be *general* creditors of the business, with no special claims on the assets of the business. If in fact the accounts payable creditors have unusual rights for payment against the business, these abnormal claims should be disclosed in the footnotes to its financial statements.

Here is another important point: Financial statement readers are entitled to assume that the accounts payable are *current*, which means that the liabilities are not seriously overdue (i.e., way beyond their due dates for payment). Suppose, for instance, that half of the company's accounts payable are two or three months overdue. In this situation the business should disclose the overdue amount in the footnotes to its financial statements.

We may not need to emphasize this, but accounts payable are noninterest-bearing and should not be intermingled with the interest-bearing debts of the business. As you see in Exhibit 7.1, interest-bearing liabilities (notes payable) are reported in separate liability accounts. By the way, long-overdue accounts payable may begin to accrue interest at the option of the creditor.

We should mention that the disclosure standards we discuss here for accounts payable are not necessarily complied within actual financial reports. You don't see much disclosure about accounts payable in business financial statements. We think a business should make full disclosure in its financial reports. But in fact companies are cut a lot of slack in the area of accounts payable. You don't find detailed information about a company's accounts payable liability in its financial statements, even though this particular liability may be more than 10 percent of a company's total assets and may be larger than its cash balance at the balance sheet date (as it is in our business example).

8

OPERATING EXPENSES AND ACCOUNTS PAYABLE

EXHIBIT 8.1—SELLING, GENERAL, AND ADMINISTRATIVE EXPENSES AND ACCOUNTS PAYABLE

Dollar Amounts in Thousands

Net cash flow from profit-making activities during year

Sales Revenue	$ 52,000
Cost of Goods Sold Expense	$(33,800)
Selling, General, and Administrative Expenses	$(12,480)
Depreciation Expense	$ (785)
Interest Expense	$ (545)
Income Tax Expense	$ (1,748)
Net Income	$ 2,642

> Assuming three weeks of annual selling, general, and administrative expenses are unpaid at the end of the year, the year-end balance of Accounts Payable for these unpaid expenses is:
>
> 3/52 × $12,480 = $720

BALANCE SHEET AT YEAR-END

ASSETS

Cash	$ 3,265
Accounts Receivable	$ 5,000
Inventory	$ 8,450
Prepaid Expenses	$ 960
Property, Plant, and Equipment	$16,500
Accumulated Depreciation	$ (4,250)
Intangible Assets	$ 5,575
Total Assets	**$35,500**

LIABILITIES AND STOCKHOLDERS' EQUITY

Accounts Payable	$2,600	
Accounts Payable	$ 720	$ 3,320
Accrued Expenses Payable		$ 1,515
Income Tax Payable		$ 165
Short-Term Notes Payable		$ 3,125
Long-Term Notes Payable		$ 4,250
Capital Stock		$ 8,125
Retained Earnings		$15,000
Total Liabilities and Stockholders' Equity		**$35,500**

Recording Expenses Before They Are Paid

Please refer to Exhibit 8.1, which highlights the connection between *selling, general, and administrative expenses* in the income statement and the second of the two *accounts payable* components in the balance sheet. Recall from Chapter 7 the two sources of accounts payable: inventory purchases on credit and expenses not paid immediately. Chapter 7 explains the connection between inventory and accounts payable. This chapter explains how expenses also drive the accounts payable liability of a business.

Every business in the world has a wide variety of operating expenses. The term *operating* does *not* include cost of goods sold, interest, and income tax expenses. In our example, the company's depreciation expense is reported separately. All other operating expenses are combined into one conglomerate account labeled "Selling, General, and Administrative Expenses." (See the income statement in Exhibit 8.1.) This expense title is widely used by businesses, although you certainly see variations.

Day in and day out, many operating expenses are recorded when they are paid, at which time an expense account is increased and the cash account is decreased. But some operating expenses have to be recorded *before* they are paid, which is the focus of this chapter.

Operating expenses is the convenient term that we use in the collective sense to refer to many different specific expenses of running (operating) a business enterprise. In this business example, the annual depreciation expense on the company's long-lived, fixed assets is shown as a separate expense. So, the $12,480,000 total amount of selling, general, and administrative expenses does not include depreciation. (It would if the depreciation expense were not reported separately.) And, to remind you, the $12,480,000 total for operating expenses does not include cost of goods sold, interest, and income tax expenses, which are reported separately in the income statement (see Exhibit 8.1 again).

Operating expenses include the following specific expenses (in no particular order):

- Rental of buildings, copiers, trucks and autos, telephone system equipment, computers, and other assets.

- Wages, salaries, commissions, bonuses, and other compensation paid to managers, office staff, salespersons, warehouse workers, security guards, and other employees. (Compensation of production employees is included in the cost of goods manufactured and becomes part of inventory cost.)

- Payroll taxes and fringe benefit costs of labor, such as health and medical plan contributions by the employer and the cost of employee retirement plans (a difficult cost to measure for defined benefit plans but not so difficult for 401(k) and other types of defined contribution plans).

- Office and data processing supplies.

- Telephone, fax, Internet, and website costs.

- Inventory shrinkage due to shoplifting and employee theft or careless handling and storage of products; the cost of goods stolen and damaged may be recorded in the cost of goods sold expense or, alternatively, classified as an operating expense.

- Liability, fire, accident, and other insurance costs.

- Utility costs of electricity and fuel.

- Advertising and sales promotion costs, which are major expenditures by many businesses.

- Bad debts, which are past-due accounts receivable that turn out to be not collectible and have to be written off.

- Transportation and shipping costs.

- Travel and entertainment costs.

This list is not all-inclusive. We're sure you could think of many more expenses of operating a business. Even relatively small businesses keep 100 or more separate accounts for specific operating expenses. Larger business corporations keep thousands of specific expense accounts. In their external financial reports, however, most publicly owned corporations report only one, two, or three operating expenses categories. For instance, advertising expenses are reported internally to managers, but you don't see this particular expense in many externally reported income statements.

As we mentioned, some operating expenses are recorded when they are paid—not before nor after. The business records an expense and decreases cash. This chapter focuses on another basic way that operating expenses are recorded—by increasing the accounts payable liability. (Following chapters explain other ways of recording operating expenses and the asset and liability accounts involved.)

It would be convenient if every dollar of operating expenses were a dollar actually paid out in the same period. But, as this and later chapters demonstrate, running a business is not so simple. The point is that for many operating expenses a business cannot wait to record the expense until it pays the expense. As soon as a liability is incurred, the amount of expense should be recorded. The term *incurred* means that the business has a definite responsibility to pay a third party, which has a legal claim against the business.

A liability is incurred when a company takes on an obligation to make future payment and has received the economic benefit of the cost in operating the business. Recording the liability for an unpaid expense is one fundamental aspect of *accrual-basis accounting*. Expenses are *accrued* (i.e., recorded before they are paid) so that the amount of each expense is deducted from sales revenue in order to measure profit correctly for the period.

For an example, suppose on December 15 a business receives an invoice from its attorneys for legal work done for the company over the previous two or three months. The end of the company's accounting (fiscal) year is December 31. The company will not pay its lawyers until next year. This cost belongs in this year, and should be recorded in the legal expense account. Therefore, the company records an increase in the accounts payable liability account to record the legal expense.

This is just one example of many; other examples include bills from newspapers for advertisements that have already appeared in the papers, telephone bills, and so on. Generally speaking, liabilities for unpaid expenses are for short credit periods, typically one month or less.

Based on its experience, a business should know the average time it takes to pay its short-term accounts payable arising from unpaid operating expenses. The average credit period of the company in our example is three weeks. Thus, the amount of its accounts payable from this source can be expressed as follows:

$$\frac{3}{52} \times \begin{array}{c} \$12,\!480,\!000 \\ \text{Operating Expenses} \\ \text{for Year} \end{array} = \begin{array}{c} \$720,\!000 \\ \text{Accounts} \\ \text{Payable} \end{array}$$

In Exhibit 8.1 note that the year-end amount for this component of accounts payable is $720,000.

Operating costs that are not paid immediately are recorded in the accounts payable liability account both to recognize the obligation of the business to make payment for these costs, and to record expenses that have benefited the operations of the business so that profit is measured correctly for the period. In other words, there is both an income statement and a balance sheet reason for recording unpaid expenses.

There's no question that accounts payable should be recorded for expenses that haven't been paid by the end of the accounting year. However, the recording of unpaid expenses does not immediately decrease cash. Actual cash outflow occurs later, when the accounts payable are paid. We discuss the cash flow aspects of making profit and the statement of cash flows in Chapter 14.

Accounting Issues

At the end of Chapter 7 we discuss the accounting issues regarding reporting accounts payable in the balance sheet. You may want to quickly review those points.

Generally speaking, there are no serious accounting problems regarding the accounts payable liability for unpaid operating expenses. The amounts that should be recorded are fairly clear in most situations. The business receives invoices (bills) for these expenses that are definite regarding the amounts owed by the business. Some of its vendors and suppliers may offer prompt payment discounts. For example, the business may have the option to deduct 2 percent if it pays the bill within 10 days. Generally, a business adopts a standard way of dealing with such discounts and follows the method consistently.

The most contentious financial reporting issue concerns disclosure of operating expenses in a company's income statement.

Suppose you were one of the stockholders in the business. Would you be satisfied with the company disclosing only one grand total for all its selling, general, and administrative expenses (as in Exhibit 2.1) or would you want more detail?

In later chapters we discuss the broad issue of adequate disclosure in financial reports. All we'll say here is that accounting standards are not very demanding regarding disclosure of expenses in externally reported financial statements. Companies can be tight-lipped if they so choose. To a certain extent there is a tug of war between the business that wants to keep its expense information away from the prying eyes of its competitors and critics, versus shareholders who want to see as much of the company's confidential expense information as possible.

9

OPERATING EXPENSES AND PREPAID EXPENSES

EXHIBIT 9.1—SELLING, GENERAL, AND ADMINISTRATIVE EXPENSES AND PREPAID EXPENSES

Dollar Amounts in Thousands

INCOME STATEMENT FOR YEAR

Sales Revenue	$ 52,000
Cost of Goods Sold Expense	$ (33,800)
Selling, General, and Administrative Expenses	$ (12,480)
Depreciation Expense	$ (785)
Interest Expense	$ (545)
Income Tax Expense	$ (1,748)
Net Income	$ 2,642

> Assuming the business has paid certain costs which will not be recorded as expenses until next year that in total equals four weeks of its annual operating expenses, the year-end balance of Prepaid Expenses is:
>
> $4/52 \times \$12{,}480 = \$960$

BALANCE SHEET AT YEAR-END

ASSETS

Cash	$ 3,265
Accounts Receivable	$ 5,000
Inventory	$ 8,450
Prepaid Expenses	$ 960
Property, Plant, and Equipment	$16,500
Accumulated Depreciation	$ (4,250)
Intangible Assets	$ 5,575
Total Assets	**$35,500**

LIABILITIES AND STOCKHOLDERS' EQUITY

Accounts Payable		$ 3,320
Accrued Expenses Payable	$1,440	
Accrued Expenses Payable	$ 75	$ 1,515
Income Tax Payable		$ 165
Short-Term Notes Payable		$ 3,125
Long-Term Notes Payable		$ 4,250
Capital Stock		$ 8,125
Retained Earnings		$15,000
Total Liabilities and Stockholders' Equity		**$35,500**

Paying Certain Operating Costs Before They Are Recorded as Expenses

Please refer to Exhibit 9.1, which highlights the connection between *selling, general, and administrative expenses* in the income statement and the *prepaid expenses* asset account in the balance sheet. This chapter explains that operating expenses generate this particular asset of a business.

The preceding chapter explains that some operating expenses are recorded before they are paid. This is done by recording a liability for the unpaid expenses. This chapter, in contrast, explains that certain operating costs are paid *before* the amounts should be recorded as expenses. In short, businesses have to prepay some of their expenses.

Insurance premiums are one example of prepaid expenses. Insurance premiums are paid in advance of the insurance policy period—which usually extends over 6 or 12 months. Other examples are office and computer supplies bought in bulk and then gradually used up over several weeks or months. Annual property taxes may be paid at the start of the tax year; these amounts should be allocated over the future months that benefit from the property taxes.

Cash outlays for prepaid costs are initially recorded in the *prepaid expenses* asset account that acts as a holding account. Then the amounts are gradually charged out over time to operating expenses. This two-step process is the means of delaying the expensing of costs to future months. The prepaid cost is allocated so that each future month receives its fair share of the cost. When the time comes, an entry is recorded to remove the appropriate portion of the cost from the prepaid expenses asset account, and the amount is entered in an operating expense account.

Based on its experience and the nature of its operations, a business knows how large, on average, the total of its prepaid expenses is relative to its annual operating expenses. In this example the company's prepaid expenses equal four weeks of its annual operating expenses. Thus, the balance in its prepaid expenses asset account can be expressed as follows:

$$\frac{4}{52} \times \begin{array}{c} \$12,480,000 \text{ Selling,} \\ \text{General, and Administrative} \\ \text{Expenses for Year} \end{array} = \begin{array}{c} \$960,000 \\ \text{Prepaid} \\ \text{Expenses} \end{array}$$

In Exhibit 9.1, notice that the year-end balance of this asset account is $960,000. Its balance is much smaller than the company's balances of accounts receivable and inventory. (This is typical for most businesses.)

Summing up, the main reason for recording operating costs that are paid in advance in the prepaid expenses asset account is to delay recording these costs as expenses until the proper time. Charging off prepayments immediately to expenses would be premature—it would be robbing Paul (expenses higher this period) to pay Peter (expenses lower next period).

The main purpose of putting prepaid operating costs into the prepaid expenses account is not to recognize an asset, although prepaid costs are a legitimate asset. In one sense, prepaying an operating expense is similar to making an investment in a long-term operating asset such as a building, or equipment and machinery. Charging off prepaid operating costs to expenses is done over a short time frame, whereas allocating the cost of a building to expense is spread out over many years (as the next chapter explains).

The prepayment of operating expenses decreases cash as soon as the check is cut. So, cash outflow takes place before the expense is recorded. An increase in the prepaid expenses asset account is bad for cash flow. (Chapter 14 presents a summary of the cash flow analysis of all expenses and sales revenue.)

Accounting Issues: Using Prepaid Expenses to Massage the Numbers

In the large majority of situations there are no serious accounting problems concerning prepaid expenses. On the other hand, we can imagine an unusual situation in which the balance in a company's prepaid expenses asset account should be written down as a loss. For instance, a business may be on the verge of collapse, and its prepaid expenses may therefore have no future benefit and may not be recoverable. In other words, accounting for prepaid expenses assumes that the business will remain a going concern in the foreseeable future. (This key assumption is made in accounting for all assets, although an imminent threat of shutting down a business would affect different assets differently.)

So far we haven't talked about *accounting fraud* and *massaging the numbers*. This is as good a place as any to open up the discussion about these dark corners of accounting. Accounting fraud is also called *cooking the books*, and massaging the numbers is also called *earnings management*. There is no bright line separating accounting fraud and massaging the numbers. Generally speaking, accounting fraud is much bigger and typically involves the falsification of sales and/or the failure to recognize the full amount of expenses.

Massaging the numbers can be viewed as "fluffing the pillows," to make the accounting numbers, and especially bottom-line profit, look a little better than it would by strictly adhering to the company's established accounting methods and procedures. Massaging the numbers is like driving a little over the speed limit. Accounting fraud is like driving while drunk and posing serious risk to others.

The prepaid expenses asset, being a relatively small asset, is generally not an important element in accounting fraud. However, the prepaid expenses asset account could easily be used for the manipulation of expenses. For example, a business may not record certain prepaid costs; instead it could record the prepayments immediately to expenses. Alternatively, a business could intentionally delay charging certain prepaid costs to expenses, even though the expenses should be recorded in this period.

Accountants, being in charge of recording revenue and expenses, are involved in any manipulation of expenses (and also revenue). But they do not take the initiative on their own in massaging the numbers. A top-level manager, either directly or indirectly, instructs the accountant to come up with more (or less) profit for the period—by whatever means it takes. In doing so the accountant has to override established accounting procedures. Needless to say, this puts the accountant in an ethical dilemma. For that matter, the heavy-handed manipulation of accounting numbers could possibly be a criminal offense. The CPA auditor of a company's financial statements should discover any significant amount of accounting manipulation.

We discuss massaging the numbers and accounting fraud at greater length in later chapters. We should point out one further thing here, that massaging the numbers for sales revenue and expenses affects both the income statement *and* the balance sheet. Manipulating the accounting numbers has a double-edged effect—both the income statement and the balance sheet include incorrect amounts.

Suppose, for instance, that some of the products in the company's ending inventory suffered uninsured damage during the year. The damaged products will be sold next year below cost. Accounting theory is clear. The loss should be recorded in the period the damage occurs. But suppose top management does not want to record the hit against profit this year. The loss can be more easily absorbed next year (they think).

So, assume that the accountant does not record the loss this year. Therefore, bottom-line profit in the income statement is too high. And, the amount of inventory in the balance sheet at the end of the year is too high. Furthermore, the retained earnings account in the balance sheet (which accumulates the profit recorded each year) is too high. Both financial statements contain deliberate errors.

Needless to say, business managers and accountants should have ethical qualms about massaging the numbers. But we can say without fear of contradiction that manipulating accounting numbers goes on all the time. Everyone condemns accounting fraud, but there is not nearly as much wrath about massaging the numbers. This is a dark corner of accounting that accountants do not like to talk about. It's like we all disapprove of lying, even though most of us do it a little ourselves.

10

DEPRECIATION EXPENSE AND PROPERTY, PLANT, AND EQUIPMENT

Overview of Expense Accounting

Before plowing into the nature of depreciation expense and its connections in the balance sheet, we offer a general review of expenses in general. Financial statement accounting is especially concerned with the *timing* of recording expenses. The main goal is to record expenses in the correct period, neither too soon nor too late, so that profit for the period is as accurate as possible.

The two guiding principles for recording expenses are:

1. *Match expenses with sales revenue:* Cost of goods sold expense, sales commissions expense, and any other expense directly connected with making particular sales are recorded in the same period as the sales revenue. This is relatively straightforward; all direct expenses of making sales should be matched against sales revenue. It would be foolhardy to put revenue in one period and the expenses of that revenue in another period. You agree, don't you?

2. *Match other expenses with the period benefited:* Many expenses are not directly identifiable with particular sales. Such *nondirect expenses* include office employees' salaries, rental of warehouse space, computer processing and accounting costs, legal and audit fees, interest on borrowed money, and many more. Nondirect expenses are just as necessary as direct expenses, but they cannot be matched with particular sales. Therefore, nondirect expenses are recorded in the period in which the benefit to the business occurs.

Chapter 6 explains the use of the inventory asset account to hold the cost of products that are manufactured or purchased until the goods are sold, at which time cost of goods expense is recorded and the inventory asset account is decreased. Chapter 8 explains the use of the accounts payable liability account to record unpaid costs that should be recorded as expenses in the current period. Chapter 9 explains the use of the prepaid expenses asset account to delay recording operating expenses until the proper time period.

This chapter explains that the costs of the long-lived operating assets of a business in theory should be recorded to expense over the span of their useful lives. These assets (with the exception of land) gradually lose their usefulness to a business over time. The allocation of the cost of a long-term operating asset to expense over the useful life of the asset is called *depreciation*. In accounting, depreciation means the multiyear *allocation* of the costs of long-term assets.

EXHIBIT 10.1—PROPERTY, PLANT, AND EQUIPMENT, DEPRECIATION EXPENSE, AND ACCUMULATED DEPRECIATION

Dollar Amounts in Thousands

BALANCE SHEET AT YEAR-END

ASSETS

Cash	$ 3,265
Accounts Receivable	$ 5,000
Inventory	$ 8,450
Prepaid Expenses	$ $960

> The costs of long-term operating assets (except land) are allocated to depreciation expense over the years of their estimated useful lives.

Property, Plant, and Equipment	$ 16,500	
Accumulated Depreciation	$ (4,250)	$12,250
Intangible Assets		$ 5,575
Total Assets		$35,500

INCOME STATEMENT FOR YEAR

Sales Revenue	$ 52,000
Cost of Goods Sold Expense	$ (33,800)
Selling, General, and Administrative Expenses	$ (12,480)
Depreciation Expense	$ (785)
Interest Expense	$ (545)
Income Tax Expense	$ (1,748)
Net Income	$ 2,642

> The amount of depreciation expense is not recorded as a decrease in the asset account. Instead it is accumulated in a *contra* or *offset* account, called Accumulated Depreciation.

LIABILITIES AND STOCKHOLDERS' EQUITY

Accounts Payable	$ 3,320
Accrued Expenses Payable	$ 1,515
Income Tax Payable	$ 165
Short-Term Notes Payable	$ 3,125
Long-Term Notes Payable	$ 4,250
Capital Stock	$ 8,125
Retained Earnings	$15,000
Total Liabilities and Stockholders' Equity	$35,500

Depreciation Expense

Please refer to Exhibit 10.1, which shows the connections between *property, plant, and equipment* in the balance sheet and *depreciation expense* in the income statement, and from depreciation expense back to *accumulated depreciation* in the balance sheet. In brief, the costs of the company's long-term operating assets are allocated (in theory) over their estimated economic lives, and the amount of the periodic depreciation expense is accumulated in a separate contra (offset) account that is deducted from the cost of the assets.

The company in this example needs certain specialized machinery, equipment, and tools that are rented under multiyear lease contracts. Legally the business doesn't own the leased assets. The monthly rents paid on these leases are charged to expenses. Leased assets are not reported in a company's balance sheet (unless the lease is essentially a method to finance the purchase of the asset). A company should disclose rental payment commitments of its long-term leases in the footnotes to its financial statements. Accounting rule-makers recently tightened lease accounting rules. More leases will have to be reported in the balance sheet as an asset with a corresponding liability for future rental payments.

The company in our example owns a variety of long-term operating assets—a production plant and office building, furniture and fixtures, computers, delivery trucks, forklifts, and automobiles used by its salespersons. The business buys these assets, uses them for several years, and eventually disposes of them. Because of their long-term nature, accountants call them *fixed assets*, although this term is not used in the formal financial statements of a business.

The long-term operating assets owned by a business usually are grouped into one inclusive account for balance sheet reporting. One common title is *Property, Plant, and Equipment*, which we use. (A detailed breakdown of fixed assets may be disclosed in a footnote to the financial statements, or in a separate schedule.) At the end of its most recent year, the business reports that the total cost of its fixed assets (property, plant, and equipment) is $16,500,000 (see Exhibit 10.1). This amount is the total of the original costs of its fixed assets, or how much they cost when the business bought them.

Fixed assets are used for several years, but eventually they wear out or lose their utility to a business. In short, these assets have a limited life span—they don't last forever. For example, delivery trucks may be driven 200,000 or 300,000 miles, but are replaced eventually.

The cost of a delivery truck, for instance, is prorated over the years of expected use to the business. How many years, exactly? A business has its experience to go on in estimating the useful lives of fixed assets. In theory, a business should make the most realistic forecast possible regarding how long each fixed asset will be used, and then spread the asset's cost over that life span. However, theory doesn't count for much on this score. Most businesses turn to the federal income tax code and regulations to determine the useful lives of their fixed assets. Those life spans are permitted for calculating the depreciation expense amounts that can be deducted in their federal income tax returns.

In the federal income tax system, every kind of fixed asset is given a minimum life over which its cost can be depreciated. The cost of land is not depreciated, on the grounds that land never wears out and has a perpetual life. (The market value of a parcel of real estate can fluctuate over time, and floods and earthquakes can destroy land, but that's another matter.)

The federal income tax permits (but does not require) *accelerated depreciation* methods. The term *accelerated* means two different things. First, for income tax, fixed assets can be depreciated over lives that are considerably *shorter* than their actual useful lives. For example, automobiles and light trucks can be depreciated over five years even though these fixed assets typically last longer than five years (except perhaps taxicabs in New York City). Buildings placed in service after 1993 can be depreciated over 39 years, but most buildings stand longer. In writing the income tax law, Congress decided that allowing businesses to depreciate their fixed assets faster than they actually wear out is good economic policy.

Second, *accelerated* means *front-loaded*, which describes a process by which more of the cost of a fixed asset is depreciated in the first half of its useful life than in its second half. Instead of a level, uniform amount of depreciation expense year to year (which is called the *straight-line* method), the income tax law allows a business to deduct higher amounts of depreciation expense in the front (early) years and less in the back (later) years.

Accelerated depreciation methods, given the imprimatur of the income tax code, are very popular. A business can reduce its taxable income in the early years of its fixed assets by choosing accelerated depreciation methods. But these effects don't necessarily mean it's the best depreciation method in theory or in actual practice.

A business must maintain a depreciation schedule for each of its fixed assets and keep track of its original cost and how much depreciation expense is recorded each year. Only cost can be depreciated. Once the total cost of a fixed asset has been depreciated, no more depreciation expense can be recorded. At that point, the fixed asset is fully depreciated, even though it still may be used several more years.

In our company example, the depreciation expense for its most recent year is $785,000 (Exhibit 10.1). Its manufacturing and office building is being depreciated by the straight-line method; its other fixed assets (e.g., trucks, computers, equipment) are being depreciated according to an accelerated method.

The amount of depreciation expense charged to each year is quite arbitrary compared with most other operating expenses. The main reason is that useful life estimates are arbitrary. For a six-month insurance policy, there's little doubt that the total premium cost should be allocated over exactly six months. But long-lived operating assets such as office desks, display shelving, file cabinets, computers, and so on present much more difficult problems. Past experience is a good guide but it leaves a lot of room for error.

Given the inherent problems of estimating useful lives, financial statement readers are well advised to keep in mind the consequences of adopting ultraconservative useful life estimates. If useful life estimates are too short (the assets are actually used many more years), then depreciation expense is recorded too quickly. Keep this point in mind. The main impact is that the balance of its fixed assets is lower that it would be if a more realistic, longer depreciation life had been adopted by the business—which also means that its total assets are reported at a lower amount in its balance sheet.

A business could keep two sets of depreciation books. It could depreciate fixed assets over short lives for income tax, and use longer, more realistic lives for financial reporting. However, most businesses use the income tax depreciation lives in their financial statements. Rapid (accelerated) depreciation is the norm in financial reporting.

Recording depreciation expense does *not*—we repeat, does *not*—decrease cash; cash is not involved in recording depreciation. Rather, recording depreciation expense has the effect of decreasing a fixed asset. To understand this point, you have to understand the accumulated depreciation account, which we explain next.

Accumulated Depreciation and Book Value of Fixed Assets

The amount of depreciation each period is *not* recorded directly as a decrease in the fixed asset account. Yet, decreasing the asset account would seem to make sense because the whole point of depreciation is to recognize the wearing out of the fixed asset over time. So, why not decrease the fixed asset account?

Well, the universal practice throughout the accounting world is to accumulate depreciation expense in a companion account called *accumulated depreciation*. This account does what its name implies—it accumulates, period by period, the amounts recorded as depreciation expense. In Exhibit 10.1, notice that the balance in this account at the end of the company's most recent year is $4,250,000.

Compared to the $16,500,000 cost of its fixed assets, the accumulated depreciation balance indicates that the company's fixed assets are not very old. Furthermore, the company recorded $785,000 depreciation expense in its most recent year. At this clip, a little more than five years' depreciation has been recorded on its property, plant, and equipment (fixed assets).

As you see in Exhibit 10.1, the balance in accumulated depreciation is deducted from the original cost of fixed assets. In our business example, the $16,500,000 cost of fixed assets minus the $4,250,000 accumulated depreciation equals $12,250,000. Cost less accumulated depreciation is referred to as the *book value* of fixed assets.

Generally the entire cost of a fixed asset is depreciated, assuming the business holds on to the asset until the end of its depreciation life. In one sense, book value represents future depreciation expense, although a business may dispose of some of its fixed assets before they are fully depreciated. (And keep in mind that the cost of land, which is included in the property, plant, and equipment account, is not depreciated.)

Finally, remember that the $4,250,000 accumulated depreciation balance is the total depreciation that has been recorded during all years the fixed assets have been used. It's not just the depreciation expense from the most recent year.

Book Values and Current Replacement Costs

After recording depreciation expense for its most recent year, the book value of the company's long-term operating (fixed) assets is $12,250,000 (see Exhibit 10.1). Suppose that the business could determine the current replacement costs at the balance sheet date of the same exact fixed assets in the same used condition. (This might not be entirely realistic.) Would you expect that the current market replacement costs would be exactly the same as the book values of the fixed assets? Chances are that the current replacement costs would be higher than the book value of the fixed assets. This would be due to general inflation and the use of accelerated depreciation methods.

The original costs of fixed assets reported in a balance sheet are not meant to be indicators of the current replacement costs of the assets. Original costs are the amounts of capital invested in the assets that should be recovered through sales revenue over the years of using the assets in the operations of the business. Depreciation accounting is a *cost-recovery–based* method—not a *mark-to-market* method. In short, fixed asset accounting does not attempt to record changes in current replacement cost.

We should point out that business managers shouldn't ignore the current replacement values of their fixed assets. Fixed assets can be destroyed or damaged by fire, flooding, riots, terrorist acts, tornadoes, explosions, and structural failure. Quite clearly, business managers should be concerned about insuring fixed assets for their current replacement costs. However, in financial reporting a business does not write up the recorded value of its fixed assets to reflect current replacement costs. (There's no rule prohibiting the disclosure of the estimated current replacement costs of its fixed assets, but businesses don't do this.)

You may encounter criticism of financial statement accounting on the grounds that depreciation expense is based on the historical cost of fixed assets instead of on current replacement costs. Someday Congress might consider changing the federal income tax law to allow replacement-cost-basis depreciation (without taxing the gain from writing up fixed assets to their higher replacement costs) but we don't forsee such a radical change.

We must admit, though, that anything is possible regarding fixed asset depreciation within the federal income tax law. For instance, we would not be surprised if Congress were to change the useful lives of fixed assets for business income tax purposes—something it has done in the past. But Congress has not been willing to abandon the actual cost basis for fixed asset depreciation.

Intangible Assets

So far in the chapter we have focused on the depreciation of *tangible* fixed assets. Many businesses also invest in *intangible* assets, which have no physical existence. You can't see or touch these assets. For example, a business may purchase a valuable patent that it will use in its production process over many years. Or a business may buy an established trademark that is well known among consumers. When a business buys patents or trademarks, the costs of these particular assets are recorded in long-term asset accounts called *Patents* and *Trademarks*, respectively.

A business may purchase another going business as a whole and pay more than the sum of its identifiable assets (minus its liabilities). Often the company to be acquired has been in business for many years and it has built up a trusted name and reputation. It may have a large list of loyal customers that will continue to buy the company's products in the future. The experience and loyalty of the acquired company's employees may be the main reason to pay for more than the identifiable assets being acquired in the purchase of the business. Or the business being bought out may have secret processes and product formulas that give it a strong competitive advantage.

There are many reasons to pay more for an established, going-concern business than just the sum of its identifiable assets (minus the liabilities being assumed when buying the business). When a business pays more than the sum of the specific assets (less liabilities) of the business being acquired, the excess is generally recorded in the asset account called *goodwill*. Whether to systematically charge off the cost of goodwill and other intangible assets has been a vexing issue over the years. We won't bore you here with an extended discussion of the various arguments.

At the present time, accounting standards do not require the systematic allocation of the cost of an intangible asset to expense (called *amortization* expense). Instead, when an intangible asset has suffered an observable loss of value, a business makes an entry to *write down* the recorded value of the intangible asset. Businesses make yearly assessments of whether their intangible assets have been impaired and, if so, record an expense for the effect of the impairment.

Based on its yearly assessment, the business in our example determined that its intangible assets did not suffer a loss of value during the year. Therefore it did not record an expense for its intangible assets. Notice in Exhibit 10.1 that there is no line of connection from the intangible assets account in the balance sheet to an expense in the income statement. Keep in mind, however, that an expense is recorded when there is a diminishment in value of a company's intangible assets.

Accounting Issues

There's a multitude of accounting problems regarding the depreciation of long-term operating assets, as well as other accounting problems concerning fixed assets. A company's fixed assets are typically a sizable part of its total assets, so these accounting problems are important.

Many books have been written on the theory of depreciation, arguing the merits of different methods. As we mention in the chapter, most businesses resort to the income tax ground rules for depreciating their fixed assets. This is a practical and expedient answer to depreciation accounting questions.

Another common issue with fixed assets is impairment. A business should write down a fixed asset if its economic value has become *impaired*. This can occur when an asset's value declines unexpectedly, so that the cost to acquire it will not be recovered. An airline, for example, could have surplus jets that it no longer needs, or a manufacturer may shut down an entire plant because of a fall-off in demand for the products made there. When a business has excess capacity, it should take a hard look at whether its fixed assets should be written down. Making write-downs of fixed assets due to loss of economic value is painful and it can put a big dent in profit, of course.

There are also accounting problems that emerge when drawing the line between the costs of routine maintenance of fixed assets and major outlays that extend the life or improve the appearance or efficiency of fixed assets. Routine maintenance costs should be expensed as they occur. The costs of major improvements should be recorded in the fixed asset account and depreciated over future years.

Insurance can pose another complication. A business may self-insure some of its fixed assets instead of buying casualty insurance coverage. But this makes the business vulnerable to huge write-offs if it suffers an actual loss. When a business self-insures its fixed assets, should it record an estimated expense each year for a future loss that hasn't yet happened, and may never happen? Most businesses do not.

In summary, there are many serious accounting problems surrounding fixed assets. Therefore, a business definitely should explain its depreciation and other fixed asset accounting policies in the footnotes to its financial statements. Also, a company should disclose how it accounts for its intangible assets, especially when it makes a major write-down in one or more of these assets during the year.

In Chapter 6 we argue that the company's cost of goods sold expense accounting method should be consistent with how the business sets sales prices. Likewise, we would argue that choosing the depreciation expense method should be guided mainly by the number of years over which the business plans to recoup the costs invested in its fixed assets through sales revenue. If the business adopts a sales pricing policy for recapturing the cost of a fixed asset over, say, 20 years, we would argue that a 20-year depreciation life should be used. But it may depreciate the cost over 10 years, as permitted by the income tax law. Talk about a mismatch between sales revenue and expenses!

11

ACCRUING LIABILITY FOR UNPAID EXPENSES

EXHIBIT 11.1—ACCRUING UNPAID EXPENSES
Dollar Amounts in Thousands

INCOME STATEMENT FOR YEAR

Sales Revenue	$ 52,000
Cost of Goods Sold Expense	$(33,800)
Selling, General, and Administrative Expenses	$(12,480)
Depreciation Expense	$ (785)
Interest Expense	$ (545)
Income Tax Expense	$ (1,748)
Net Income	$ 2,642

Assuming six weeks of the year's total of selling, general, and administrative expenses is unpaid at year-end, the amount payable for these operating expenses is: 6/52 × $12,480 = $1,440

A small amount of the annual interest expense is unpaid at year-end, which is recorded to recognize the full amount of interest expense for the year.

BALANCE SHEET AT YEAR-END

ASSETS

Cash	$ 3,265
Accounts Receivable	$ 5,000
Inventory	$ 8,450
Prepaid Expenses	$ 960
Property, Plant, and Equipment	$16,500
Accumulated Depreciation	$ (4,250)
Intangible Assets	$ 5,575
Total Assets	$35,500

LIABILITIES AND STOCKHOLDERS' EQUITY

Accounts Payable		$ 3,320
Accrued Expenses Payable	$1,440	
Accrued Expenses Payable	$ 75	$ 1,515
Income Tax Payable		$ 165
Short-Term Notes Payable		$ 3,125
Long-Term Notes Payable		$ 4,250
Capital Stock		$ 8,125
Retained Earnings		$15,000
Total Liabilities and Stockholders' Equity		$35,500

Recording Accrued Liability for Operating Expenses

Please refer to Exhibit 11.1, which highlights the connections between *selling, general, and administrative expenses* in the income statement and the *accrued expenses payable* liability in the balance sheet, and between *interest expense* in the income statement and the same liability in the balance sheet. You get two for the price of one in this chapter. Both connections are based on the same idea—unpaid expenses at year-end are recorded so that the full, correct amount of expense is recognized in measuring profit for the year.

Chapter 8 explains that a business records certain expenses as soon as the bills (invoices) are received for these operating costs, even though it doesn't pay the bills until weeks later. This chapter explains that a business has to go looking for certain unpaid expenses at the end of the period. No bills or invoices are received for these expenses; they build up, or *accrue*, over time.

For instance, the business in our example pays its salespersons commissions based on their individual sales each month. Commissions are calculated at the end of each month, but are not paid until the following month. At year-end, the sales commissions earned for the final month of the year have not been paid. To record this expense, the company makes an entry in the liability account *accrued expenses payable*, which is a different sort of liability than accounts payable.

The accountant should know which expenses accumulate over time and make the appropriate calculations for these unpaid amounts at year-end. A business does not receive an invoice (bill) for these expenses from an outside vendor or supplier. A business has to generate its own internal invoices to itself, as it were. Its accounting department must be especially alert to which specific expenses need to be accrued.

In addition to sales commissions payable, a business has several other accrued expenses that should be recorded at the end of the period. The following are typical examples:

- Accumulated vacation and sick leave pay owed to employees, which can add up to a sizable amount.

- Partial-month telephone and electricity costs that have been incurred but not yet billed to the company.

- Property taxes that should be charged to the year, but the business has not received the tax bill by the end of the year.

- Warranty and guarantee work on products already sold that will be done in the future; the sales revenue has been recorded this year, so these post sale expenses also should be recorded in the same period to match all expenses with sales revenue.

Failure to record accrued liabilities for unpaid expenses could cause serious errors in a company's annual financial statements—liabilities would be understated in its balance sheet and expenses would be understated in its income statement for the year. A business definitely should identify which expenses accumulate over time and record the appropriate amounts of these liabilities at the end of the year.

In this example, the average period before the company pays certain operating expenses is six weeks. Thus, the amount of its accrued operating expenses payable at the end of the year can be expressed as follows:

$$\frac{6}{52} \times \begin{array}{c} \$12,480,000 \text{ Selling,} \\ \text{General, and Administrative} \\ \text{Expenses for Year} \end{array} = \begin{array}{c} \$1,440,000 \\ \text{Accrued Expenses} \\ \text{Payable} \end{array}$$

See in Exhibit 11.1 that the ending balance of accrued expenses payable includes $1,440,000 for operating expenses. Is six weeks right for a typical business? Well, it's difficult to generalize from business to business. We'd say that six weeks is more or less average, but keep in mind that every business is different.

We might mention that it is not unusual that the ending balance of a company's accrued expenses payable is larger than its accounts payable for unpaid operating expenses. In our business example, the ending balance of its accounts payable for operating expenses is $720,000 (from Exhibit 8.1), which is only half as much as its $1,440,000 accrued expenses payable at the end of the year.

Speaking of accounts payable, some businesses merge accrued expenses payable with accounts payable and report only one liability in their external balance sheets. Both types of liabilities are noninterest-bearing. Both emerge out of the operations of the business, and from manufacturing or purchasing products. For this reason they are sometimes called *spontaneous liabilities*, which means they arise on the spot—not from borrowing money, but from operating the business. Grouping both types of liabilities in one account is acceptable under financial reporting standards, although many companies report them separately.

The changes of accounts payable and accrued expenses can have significant impacts on cash flow, which we explain in Chapter 14. The changes in the balances of these two liabilities have cash flow impacts that are important to understand.

Bringing Interest Expense Up to Snuff

Virtually all businesses have liabilities for accounts payable and accrued expenses payable—which are part and parcel of carrying on its operations. And many businesses borrow money from a bank or from other sources. A note or similar legal instrument is signed when borrowing; hence, the liability account is called *notes payable*. Interest is paid on borrowed money (notes), whereas no interest is paid on accounts payable (unless the amount is seriously past due and an interest penalty is added by the creditor). Notes payable always are reported separately and not mixed with noninterest-bearing liabilities.

Interest is a charge per day for the use of borrowed money. Each and every day that money is borrowed increases the amount of interest owed to the lender. The ratio of interest to the amount borrowed is called the *interest rate* and it is stated as a percent. Percent means "per hundred." If you borrow $100,000 for one year and pay $6,000 interest for the use of the money for one year, the interest rate is:

$6,000 Interest ÷ $100,000 Borrowed
= $6 Per $100, or 6.0% Annual Interest Rate

Interest rates are stated as annual rates, even though the term of a loan can be shorter or longer than one year.

Interest is reported as a separate expense in income statements. It's not the size of the interest expense, but rather the special nature of interest that requires separate disclosure. Interest is a *financial* expense, as opposed to an operating expense. Interest depends on how the business is financed, which refers to the company's mix of capital sources. The basic choice is between debt capital and equity (the generic term for all kinds of ownership capital).

You may ask: When is interest paid? It depends. On short-term notes (one year or less), interest is commonly paid in one amount at the maturity date of the note, which is the last day of the loan period, at which time the amount borrowed and the accumulated interest are due. On long-term notes payable (longer than one year), interest is paid semiannually, or possibly monthly or quarterly. In any case, on both short-term and long-term notes there is a lag or delay in paying interest. Nevertheless, interest expense should be recorded for all days the money has been borrowed.

The accumulated amount of unpaid interest expense at the end of the accounting period is calculated and recorded in an accrued expenses payable type of account. In Exhibit 11.1, accrued interest payable at year-end is the second component of the accrued expenses payable liability. In our example, the amount of unpaid interest expense at year-end is fairly small, only $75,000. Generally speaking, accrued interest payable is not reported as a separate liability in external financial statements, although there is no rule against it.

Accounting Issues

One accounting issue concerns what to include in interest expense. In addition to interest paid to lenders, borrowing involves other types of costs to the business, such as loan application and processing fees, so-called points charged by lenders, and other incidental costs such as legal fees. Generally, most businesses put such extra charges in an operating expense account. So, the interest expense in the income statement is just that—the interest on its debts for the period.

The larger accounting issue concerns the accrual of operating costs—and there are many such costs. We have to tell you that the accrual of the liability for unpaid expenses depends on the good faith of the business in doing the calculations of these amounts—many of which involve arbitrary estimates and forecasts. This step in the accounting process can be easily used for *massaging the numbers*. This pejorative phrase refers to the deliberate manipulation of amounts recorded for sales revenue and expenses in order to record a higher (or lower) amount of profit for the period. (See also our discussion of this unsavory topic in Chapter 9.)

All we can do here is caution you that some businesses lay a heavy hand on the amounts recorded in their sales revenue and expense accounts, in order to smooth profit year to year or to give the profit for the year an artificial boost. Of course, these companies do not disclose in their financial statements that they have manipulated their accounting numbers to nudge profit up (or down).

As we alluded to earlier in the chapter, accrued interest payable usually is not reported as a separate liability in a company's year-end balance sheet. However, if this particular liability were large, it very well should be reported separately in the balance sheet. If a business is seriously behind in paying interest on its debts, the liability for unpaid interest should be prominently reported in its balance sheet, to call attention to this situation.

This last comment segues into the messy topic regarding how to present the financial statements of a business that is in serious financial trouble and is in default on its debt. One basic premise of financial statement accounting is the *going concern assumption*. The accountant assumes that, unless there is clear evidence to the contrary, the business will continue to operate in a normal manner and will not be forced into involuntary termination and liquidation of its assets. When a company is in serious default on its debt obligations, the creditors have the right to enforce their claims and, in extreme cases, shut the business down.

To stave off the drastic effects from unpaid creditors who may force it to shut down, the business can file for bankruptcy protection. This is a complicated area of law, way beyond the scope of this book. If there is a serious threat of such legal actions by creditors against the business, the financial statements should make full disclosure of its precarious situation.

12

INCOME TAX EXPENSE AND ITS LIABILITY

EXHIBIT 12.1—INCOME TAX EXPENSE AND INCOME TAX PAYABLE
Dollar Amounts in Thousands

INCOME STATEMENT FOR YEAR

Sales Revenue	$ 52,000
Cost of Goods Sold Expense	$ (33,800)
Selling, General, and Administrative Expenses	$ (12,480)
Depreciation Expense	$ (785)
Interest Expense	$ (545)
Income Tax Expense	$ (1,748)
Net Income	$ 2,642

> A relatively small amount of the income tax expense for the year is unpaid at year-end, which is recorded in the Income Tax Payable liability account.

BALANCE SHEET AT YEAR-END

ASSETS

Cash	$ 3,265
Accounts Receivable	$ 5,000
Inventory	$ 8,450
Prepaid Expenses	$ 960
Property, Plant, and Equipment	$ 16,500
Accumulated Depreciation	$ (4,250)
Intangible Assets	$ 5,575
Total Assets	$ 35,500

LIABILITIES AND STOCKHOLDERS' EQUITY

Accounts Payable	$ 3,320
Accrued Expenses Payable	$ 1,515
Income Tax Payable	$ 165
Short-Term Notes Payable	$ 3,125
Long-Term Notes Payable	$ 4,250
Capital Stock	$ 8,125
Retained Earnings	$ 15,000
Total Liabilities and Stockholders' Equity	$ 35,500

Taxation of Business Profit

Please refer to Exhibit 12.1, which highlights the connection between *income tax expense* in the income statement and the *income tax payable* liability in the balance sheet. Initially, income tax expense is increased and the income tax liability is increased. The tax liability account is decreased as cash payments are made. Typically, not all of the income tax expense for the year is paid by the end of the year. In this company example, a small part of the company's total income tax expense for the year, which is based on its *taxable income* for the year, has not been paid at year-end. This remaining balance will be paid in the near future. The unpaid portion stays in the company's income tax payable liability account until paid.

The business in our example is *incorporated*, meaning the business selected this form of legal organization (instead of a partnership or limited liability company). A corporation, being a separate person in the eyes of the law, has several important advantages. However, profit-motivated business corporations have one serious disadvantage. They are subject to federal and state income tax on their profits, or, to be more accurate, they owe tax based on their *taxable income*, which is earnings before income tax.

The business in this example is a regular, or so-called *C corporation*. This type of income tax entity is subject to double taxation of business profit—first in the hands of the business corporation, and second in the hands of its stockholders (but only to the extent that net income after income tax is distributed as cash dividends to them). Other types of legal business entities avoid the double taxation feature, but all their annual taxable income passes through to their owners who have to include their respective shares of the company's taxable income with their other sources of taxable income.

The first point to keep in mind is that a business corporation must earn *taxable income* to owe income tax. The simplest way to pay no income tax is to have no taxable income, or to have a loss for tax purposes. A business wants to earn profit, but earning a profit comes with the burden of sharing pretax profit with Uncle Sam and with the states that levy a tax on business profit earned within their jurisdiction.

A second point to keep in mind is that there are many loopholes and options in the federal income tax code—to say nothing about state income tax laws—that reduce or postpone income tax. The federal income tax law is complex, to say the least. (That's an understatement, if we've ever heard one.)

It takes thousands of pages of tax law to define taxable income. Most businesses use income tax professionals to help them determine their taxable income, and to advise them how to minimize the income taxes they must pay. In any one year, a business might take advantage of several different features of the tax code to minimize its taxable income for the year, or to shift taxable income to future years.

For our business example, we simplify. The business pays both federal and state income taxes based on its taxable income. Furthermore, we assume in the example that the accounting methods used to prepare its income statement are the same methods used to determine its annual taxable income. In this example, the company's earnings before income tax is $4,390,000. (You can refer back to Exhibit 2.1 to check this.) We assume that this amount is its taxable income for the year. As you see in Exhibit 12.1, the income tax is $1,748,000, which is about 40 percent of taxable income. (Keep in mind that the business pays both federal and state income taxes.)

The federal income tax law requires that a business make installment payments during the year so that close to 100 percent of its annual income tax should be paid by the end of the tax year. Actually, a relatively small fraction of the total annual income tax may not be paid by year-end without any penalty (although this can get very complicated).

The company in this example paid most of its income taxes during the year. At year-end it still owes the federal and state tax authorities only $165,000 of its annual income tax. The unpaid portion is reported in the *income tax payable* liability account, as you see in Exhibit 12.1.

The federal income tax law changes year to year. Congress is always tinkering with or, shall we say, *fine-tuning* the tax code. Old loopholes are shut down; new loopholes open up. Tax rates change over time. For these reasons the fraction of annual income tax that is unpaid at year-end is hard to predict. However, if the year-end income tax liability were a large fraction of the income tax expense for the year, we'd advise you to take a closer look.

Accounting Issues

A business may opt to determine its annual taxable income using certain accounting methods that are different from those used to report sales revenue and expenses in its income statement. Financial reporting standards require that the amount of income tax expense in the income statement be consistent with the amount of earnings before income tax in the income statement. The idea is to recognize a "normal" amount of income tax expense relative to the sales revenue and expenses above the income tax expense line. This normal amount of income tax is deducted to determine bottom-line net income after income tax.

Suppose a business reports $10,000,000 earnings before income tax in its income statement, and that the normal income tax would be $3,500,000 on this amount of taxable income. However, the business uses different accounting methods for income tax, and its actual income tax owed for the year is only, say, $2,500,000. Suppose that this difference is only temporary and will eventually reverse itself such that in future years the business will owe more income tax than will be reported in its future income statements.

In this situation the business records the full $3,500,000 amount of income tax, even though it owes only $2,500,000 for the year. The additional $1,000,000 needed to get the income tax expense up to the full $3,500,000 normal amount is recorded in a *deferred income tax liability* account—on the grounds that sooner or later the business will have to pay the additional $1,000,000 to the government.

We should tell you that there are many other problems in reporting income tax expense and income tax liabilities in business financial statements. These topics are very technical and beyond the scope of this book.

A company's financial report should include a schedule reconciling the actual income tax owed for the year (based on taxable income for the year) with the normal income tax expense reported in the income statement. We regret to tell you that this is one of the most difficult schedules you'll find in financial reports.

Accounting for income tax expense is an example of the *conditional* and *tentative* nature of financial statements. The numbers reported in financial statements might seem to be the final word on profit performance for the year and financial condition at the end of the year. But, in fact, financial statements are always provisional and subject to later revision.

The amount of income tax expense recorded for the year and the corresponding balance sheet liability are subject to revision after the close of the year. The Internal Revenue Service (IRS) may have disagreements with the income tax returns filed by the business. Indeed, the IRS may do a full-scale audit and have many disagreements.

Some businesses push the envelope in interpreting the income tax law for determining annual taxable income. Or, a business may play it straight in how it reads the law. Even so, the income tax law is complex and not clear-cut on many points. In short, there's always the possibility that the IRS may claim more income tax (or perhaps even make a refund).

13

NET INCOME AND RETAINED EARNINGS, AND EARNINGS PER SHARE (EPS)

Net Income into Retained Earnings

Exhibit 13.1 highlights the connection from *net income* in the income statement to *retained earnings* in the balance sheet, and from net income to a piece of information that we show for the first time, *earnings per share* (EPS). In short, this chapter explains that earning profit increases the retained earnings account. Then, we introduce earnings per share (EPS).

EXHIBIT 13.1—NET INCOME AND RETAINED EARNINGS; EARNINGS PER SHARE (EPS)

Dollar Amounts in Thousands, Except Earnings per Share

BALANCE SHEET AT YEAR-END

ASSETS

Cash	$ 3,265
Accounts Receivable	$ 5,000
Inventory	$ 8,450
Prepaid Expenses	$ 960
Property, Plant, and Equipment	$16,500
Accumulated Depreciation	$ (4,250)
Intangible Assets	$ 5,575
Total Assets	$35,500

INCOME STATEMENT FOR YEAR

Sales Revenue	$ 52,000
Cost of Goods Sold Expense	$ (33,800)
Selling, General, and Administrative Expenses	$ (12,480)
Depreciation Expense	$ (785)
Interest Expense	$ (545)
Income Tax Expense	$ (1,748)
Net Income	$ 2,642
Earnings per Share	$ 3.30

Bottom-line profit, or net income increases the Retained Earnings owners' equity account. (This account is decreased by dividends paid to shareholders.)

LIABILITIES AND STOCKHOLDERS' EQUITY

Accounts Payable	$ 3,320
Accrued Expenses Payable	$ 1,515
Income Tax Payable	$ $165
Short-Term Notes Payable	$ 3,125
Long-Term Notes Payable	$ 4,250
Capital Stock (800,000 shares)	$ 8,125
Retained Earnings	$15,000
Total Liabilities and Stockholders' Equity	$35,500

Suppose a business has $10 million total assets and $3 million total liabilities (including both noninterest-bearing operating liabilities such as accounts payable and interest-bearing notes payable). Over the years, its owners invested $4 million capital in the business. Therefore, liabilities plus capital from owners provide a total of $7 million of the company's total assets. Where did the other $3 million of assets come from?

Assets don't just drop down like manna from heaven. All assets have a source, and one job of accountants is to keep track of the sources of assets of the business. The source of the other $3 million in assets must be from profit the business earned but did not distribute. This is called *retained earnings*.

Two basic types of owners' equity accounts are needed for every business—one for capital invested by the owners and one for retained earnings. In our example, the business is organized legally as a corporation, and issues *capital stock shares* to its owners when they invest money in the business. As you see in Exhibit 13.1 the company uses the account called *Capital Stock* to record the investment of money by stockholders in the business.

Whenever a business distributes money to its owners, it must distinguish between returning capital they have invested in the business (which is not taxable to them) and dividing profit among them (which is taxable). A business corporation is required to keep separate accounts for capital stock and retained earnings, as you see in Exhibit 13.1.

The income statement reports that the business earned $2,642,000 in bottom-line profit, or net income for the year (see Exhibit 13.1). Net income is recorded as an increase in the retained earnings account. The retained earnings account is so named because annual profit is entered as an increase in the account, and distributions to owners from profit are entered as decreases in the account.

During the year, the business paid $750,000 total cash dividends from net income to its stockholders. Therefore, its retained earnings increased only $1,892,000 during the year, calculated as follows: $2,642,000 net income – $750,000 dividends = $1,892,000 net increase in retained earnings. At the end of the year, its retained earnings balance stands at $15,000,000, which is the cumulative result from all years the company has been in existence.

Notice in this example that the company has a relatively large retained earnings balance compared with its total assets and other balance sheet accounts. This signals that the business has been profitable in the past. However, we can't tell from the balance sheet whether the company suffered a loss one or more years in the past. By the way, if a company's losses over the years were larger than its profits, its retained earnings account would have a *negative* balance, which generally is called *accumulated deficit* (or something similar).

Many people, even some experienced business managers, are confused about what retained earnings refers to. They mistakenly imagine that retained earnings refers to a cache of cash that has been set aside. No, a thousand times no! The balance of the retained earnings account does not refer to any particular asset and certainly not to cash. Yet, we can see that the title of this balance sheet owners' equity account could mislead people into thinking that it refers to money that the business has squirreled away.

Perhaps the best way to reinforce the correct meaning of retained earnings is to rearrange the accounting equation to put emphasis on retained earnings:

$$\text{Assets} - \text{Liabilities} - \text{Capital Invested by Owner} = \text{Retained Earnings}$$

In other words, if you subtract the amount of liabilities and capital invested by owners, the remainder of assets must be attributable to earnings that have been retained in the business. In our business example the numbers (in thousands) are as follows:

$35,500 Assets – $12,375 Liabilities – $8,125 Capital Stock
= $15,000 Retained Earnings

In short, the balance in retained earnings explains one source of the total assets of a business. Making profit and keeping it in the business has added $15,000,000 to the total assets of the business in our example. You must look in the asset section of the balance sheet to see which particular assets the business owns. You can't tell a thing about which assets the business has by looking at the balance of its retained earnings. You're on the wrong side of the balance sheet.

When a business retains some (or all) of its annual net income, the retained profit should be considered as an addition to the ongoing capital base of the business. Businesses do not generally go back and pay a dividend from prior years' profits—although when a business piles up a huge cash hoard and has no other investment uses for the money, it may make a large distribution out of retained earnings.

Looking down the road to the wind-up of a business—after closing its doors, liquidating all of its assets, and paying off all of its liabilities—the business would distribute its remaining cash balance to its shareowners. The first layer of this final cash distribution to its shareowners is return of the capital they invested in the business. The remaining amount would be the final dividend (which is taxable).

Earnings per Share (EPS)

Net income, the bottom line in the income statement, is the profit measure for the business as a whole. Earnings per share (EPS) is the profit measure for each ownership unit, or for each share of capital stock of a business corporation.

Suppose in our example that you own 16,000 shares, or exactly 2 percent of the 800,000 shares of capital stock issued by the business. Several years ago you purchased these shares by investing $120,000 in the business, when it was just starting up. You're one of the original stockholders. Your $120,000 capital investment divided by your 16,000 shares means that your cost is $7.50 per share. Later investors paid more per share.

We can tell this from the company's balance sheet (see Exhibit 13.1). The $8,125,000 balance in the company's capital stock account divided by the 800,000 capital stock shares outstanding works out to an average of more than $10 per share. The later investors paid more per share than you did.

Owning only 2 percent of the total capital stock shares outstanding, you are a passive, outside investor in the business. You do not participate actively in managing the company. Of course you're entitled to 2 percent of any cash dividends paid from profit, and you control 2 percent of the votes on matters that have to be put to a vote of stockholders.

As a stockholder you are provided a copy of the company's annual (and quarterly) financial reports. Needless to say, you're very interested in the company's profit performance. You could take the view that 2 percent of annual net income "belongs" to you, which is a $52,840 slice of the company's total $2,642,000 net income. This is your cut of the net income pie. Or you could look at earnings per share (EPS), which is net income divided by the average number of capital stock shares outstanding during the year. In this example, EPS for the year just ended works out to $3.30 per share. Relative to your $7.50 cost per share you're earning a handsome return on your original investment in the business.

Earnings per share (EPS) is an especially important number for *public* companies whose capital stock shares are traded on securities exchanges. In fact, public companies must report EPS at the bottom of their income statements. Nonpublic companies do not have to report EPS although they may elect to do so (but we don't think many do).

Here, we'll just mention that EPS plays the key role in putting a market value on a share of stock in a business. For example, suppose we offer to buy 1,000 of your shares. You might offer to sell them at 15 times the stock's $3.30 EPS, or $49.50 per share. We might not be willing to pay this price, of course. In any case, it's an important point of reference. Earnings per share of public companies get a lot of attention in the press.

Accounting Issues

Accounting problems don't concern retained earnings as such, but they can impact sales revenue and expenses that determine profit for the period, which we've explained over the last several chapters. If net income is incorrect, then the retained earnings amount is incorrect.

There are some technical aspects of retained earnings, which are beyond the scope of this book. By and large, the financial reporting of retained earnings is straightforward and noncontroversial, but reporting EPS is another matter altogether. There are several problems in calculating EPS. To start with, many companies have to report not just one, but two figures for EPS—one based on the actual number of stock shares outstanding (in the hands of shareowners) and a second EPS that includes additional shares that the business is potentially committed to issue in the future. Before we close the book on retained earnings we should briefly mention another component of owners' equity called *other comprehensive income*.

You see other comprehensive income (or an equivalent title) in the financial reports of many public companies. This element of owners' equity is reported separately from retained earnings. It accumulates certain types of gains and losses recorded on the assets of a business. One example is gains and losses from changes in foreign exchange ratios that haven't yet been executed by the business but affect the value of certain of its assets.

You would think that all asset gains and losses should pass through the income statement. However, these special income and loss items bypass the income statement and are recorded directly in the owners' equity account. The thinking behind this treatment is that these peculiar gains and losses should not be included in the calculation of net income. Such gains and losses are included in a separate schedule or statement of changes in owners' equity for the year.

14

CASH FLOW FROM OPERATING (PROFIT-SEEKING) ACTIVITIES

Profit Versus Cash Flow from Profit

At this point we shift gears. Earlier chapters focus on how sales revenue and each expense in the income statement is connected with its corresponding asset or liability in the balance sheet. You can't understand a balance sheet too well without understanding how sales revenue and expenses drive many of the assets and liabilities in the balance sheet. In this chapter we focus on how the changes in these assets and liabilities during the period determine cash flow from net income (profit) for the period.

This chapter is the first of two that further explain the *statement of cash flows*. This cash flows statement is one of the three primary financial statements reported by businesses, in addition to their income statement and balance sheet. Exhibit 14.1 presents the statement of cash flows for the business we have discussed since Chapter 1. Please take a moment to read this statement from top to bottom. We'll make you a wager here. We bet you understand the second and third sections of the statement (*investing* activities and *financing* activities) better than the first section (*operating* activities). Indeed, your reaction to the first section might be that it's all Greek to you.

EXHIBIT 14.1—CASH FLOW FROM OPERATING (PROFIT-MAKING) ACTIVITIES

BALANCE SHEET	Start of Year	End of Year	Change
Assets			
Cash	$ 3,735	$ 3,265	$ (470)
Accounts Receivable	4,680	5,000	320
Inventory	7,515	8,450	935
Prepaid Expenses	685	960	275
Property, Plant, and Equipment	13,450	16,500	3,050
Accumulated Depreciation	(3,465)	(4,250)	(785)
Intangible Assets	5,000	5,575	575
Total Assets	$31,600	$35,500	
Liabilities and Stockholders' Equity			
Accounts Payable	$ 2,675	$ 3,320	645
Accrued Expenses Payable	1,035	1,515	480
Income Tax Payable	82	165	83
Short-Term Notes Payable	3,000	3,125	125
Long-Term Notes Payable	3,750	4,250	500
Capital Stock	7,950	8,125	175
Retained Earnings	13,108	15,000	1,892
Total Liabilities			
and Stockholders' Equity	$31,600	$35,500	

STATEMENT OF CASH FLOWS FOR YEAR		
Net Income—See Income Statement		$ 2,642
Accounts Receivable Increase		(320)
Inventory Increase		(935)
Prepaid Expenses Increase		(275)
Depreciation Expense		785
Accounts Payable Increase		645
Accrued Expenses Payable Increase		480
Income Tax Payable Increase		83
Cash Flow from Operating Activities		$3,105
Investments in Property, Plant, and Equipment	$(3,050)	
Investments in Intangible Assets	(575)	
Cash Flow from Investing Activities		(3,625)
Increase in Short-Term Notes Payable	$ 125	
Increase in Long-Term Notes Payable	500	
Issue of Additional Capital Stock Shares	175	
Cash Dividends Paid Shareholders	(750)	
Cash Flow from Financing Activities		50
Decrease in Cash During Year		$ (470)

Exhibit 14.1 lists the balance sheet accounts of the company at the start and end of the year and includes a column for changes. (You might compare the informal balance sheet here with the formal layout of the balance sheet introduced in Exhibit 2.2.) This chapter focuses on the first section of the cash flows statement, which explains the determinants of the company's cash flow from operating activities (i.e., its *profit-making, or profit-seeking* activities) during the year. Cash flow from operating activities is driven by changes during the period in the assets and liabilities affected by the revenue and expenses.

The main question on everyone's mind seems to be: why doesn't profit simply equal cash flow? In our example, the company earned $2,642,000 net income over the year just ended. Why didn't earning this amount of profit generate the same amount of cash flow? The first section in the cash flows statement provides the answer to this question. It shows us that the company generated $3,105,000 cash flow from profit compared with its $2,642,000 net income for the year. Cash flow from profit is quite a bit higher than net income for the period.

Business managers have a double duty—first to earn profit, and second to convert the profit into cash as soon as possible. Waiting too long to turn profit into cash reduces its value because of the time value of money. Business managers should be clear on the difference between profit reported in the income statement and the amount of cash flow from profit during the year. Creditors and investors also should keep an eye on cash flow from profit (operating activities) and management's ability to control this important number.

Changes in Assets and Liabilities That Impact Cash Flow from Operating Activities

To get from net income to the resultant cash flow, we have to make *adjustments* to net income. The adjustments are triggered by changes during the year in the company's operating assets and liabilities (i.e., the assets and liabilities directly involved in recording sales revenue and expenses). Such adjustments are listed in the statement of cash flows, just after the net income. We look at these adjustments in the order shown in the company's statement of cash flows.

Changes in operating assets and liabilities affecting operating cash flow

1. *Accounts receivable:* At year-end the company had $5,000,000 uncollected sales revenue, which is the ending balance of its accounts receivable. The $5,000,000 is included in sales revenue for determining profit, but the company did not receive this amount of cash from customers. The $5,000,000 is still in accounts receivable instead of cash at year-end. However, the company collected its $4,680,000 beginning balance of accounts receivable. The $4,680,000 collected minus $5,000,000 not collected results in a $320,000 negative impact on cash flow. See the first adjustment in the cash flows statement (Exhibit 14.1). In short, an increase in accounts receivable hurts cash flow from profit.

2. *Inventory:* Notice the rather large increase in the company's inventory during the year. This may or may not have been a smart business decision. Perhaps the business needed a larger inventory to meet higher sales demand, or maybe not. In any case, the $935,000 inventory increase has a negative impact on cash flow. The quickest way to explain this is that inventory is an investment in both products that are in the process of being manufactured and those that are finished and being held for sale. Increasing an investment means putting more money into the investment. See the second adjustment in the cash flow statement. In short, an increase in inventory hurts cash flow from operating activities.

3. *Prepaid expenses:* During the year, the company paid $960,000 for certain operating costs that will benefit next year, and therefore were not charged to expenses during the year. See the ending balance in the company's prepaid expenses account. The company paid $960,000 on top of its operating expenses for the year. But the company had $685,000 of prepaid expenses at the start of the year. Those costs were paid last year and then charged to operating expenses in the year just ended. Taking into account both the beginning and ending balances in prepaid expenses, the company experiences a $275,000 drain on cash during the year. The $685,000 not paid minus $960,000 paid has a

$275,000 negative impact on cash flow. See the third adjustment in the cash flows statement (Exhibit 14.1).

4. **Depreciation:** During the year the company recorded a $785,000 depreciation expense, not by writing a check for this amount but by writing down the cost of its property, plant, and equipment. This write-down is recorded as an increase in the accumulated depreciation account, which is the contra or offset account deducted from the property, plant, and equipment asset account. These long-term operating assets are partially written down each year to record the wear and tear on them during every year of use. The company paid cash for the assets when it bought these long-term resources. The company does not have to pay for them a second time when it uses them. In short, depreciation expense is not a cash outlay in the year recorded and therefore is a positive adjustment, or so-called add-back for determining cash flow from profit. See the fourth adjustment in the cash flow statement.

The depreciation add-back to net income can be explained another way. For the sake of argument here, assume all sales revenue had been collected in cash during the year. Part of this cash inflow from customers pays the company for the use of its long-term operating assets during the year. In setting its sales prices, a business includes depreciation as a cost of doing business. In this sense, the business sells a fraction of its fixed assets to its customers each year. As a result, each year a business recovers part of the capital invested in its fixed assets in cash flow from sales revenue. In short, the company in this example recaptured $785,000 of the investment in its property, plant, and equipment assets, which is a significant source of cash flow.

5. **Accounts payable:** The ending balance in the company's accounts payable liability reveals that manufacturing costs, product purchases, and operating expenses were not fully paid during the year. The ending balance in this liability relieved the company of making cash payments in the amount of $3,320,000 (again see Exhibit 14.1). Not paying these costs avoids cash outflow. Consider the other side of the coin, as well. The company started the year with $2,675,000 accounts payable. These liabilities were paid during the year. The $3,320,000 not paid minus $2,675,000 paid has a net $645,000 positive impact on cash flow. See the fifth adjustment in the cash flow statement.

6. **Accrued expenses payable:** This liability works the same way as accounts payable. The company did not pay $1,515,000 of its expenses during the year, which is the balance in this liability at the end of the year. But the company did pay the $1,035,000 beginning amount of this liability. The $1,515,000 not paid minus $1,035,000 paid has a net $480,000 positive impact on cash flow. See the sixth adjustment in the cash flow statement.

7. **Income tax payable:** At the start of the year, the business owed the tax authorities $82,000 on taxable income from the previous year. This amount was paid early in the year. At the end of the year, the business owed $165,000 of its income tax expense for the year; this amount was not paid. The net effect is that the company paid $83,000 less to the government than its income tax expense for the year. See the positive adjustment for the increase in income tax payable in the cash flow statement.

Summing up the seven cash flow adjustments to net income:

- Increases in operating assets cause decreases in cash flow from profit; and decreases in operating assets result in increases in cash flow from profit.

- Increases in operating liabilities help cash flow from profit; and decreases in operating liabilities result in decreases in cash flow from profit.

See in Exhibit 14.1 that the combined net effect of the seven adjustments is that cash flow from profit is $3,105,000, which is $463,000 more than profit for the year. This difference between cash flow and bottom-line profit is due to the changes in the company's operating assets and liabilities. In summary, the business realized $3,105,000 cash flow from its operating activities during the year. This source of cash flow is vital to every business.

The Direct Method for Reporting Cash Flow from Operating Activities

The accounting profession's rule-making body in the United States, the Financial Accounting Standards Board (FASB), has expressed a preference regarding the reporting of cash flow from operating activities. You might be surprised that the format you see in Exhibit 14.1 is *not* the preferred method. What you see in Exhibit 14.1 is called the *indirect method*, which uses changes in operating assets and liabilities to adjust net income, determining cash flow from operating activities. Instead, the FASB prefers the *direct method* for this section of the statement of cash flows.

Exhibit 14.2 shows the *direct method* format for reporting cash flow from operating activities. In this format, the cash flow amounts are calculated directly from sales revenue and for expenses (as opposed to being calculated from net income). The direct method format is supplemented with a schedule that summarizes the changes in operating assets and liabilities, similarly to how the changes are presented by the indirect method shown in Exhibit 14.1.

Both formats report the same cash flow from operating activities. Although the FASB expresses a clear preference for the direct

EXHIBIT 14.2—DIRECT METHOD FORMAT FOR REPORTING CASH FLOW FROM OPERATING ACTIVITIES IN THE STATEMENT OF CASH FLOWS
Dollar Amounts in Thousands

Sales Revenue	$ 51,680
Cost of Goods Sold Expense	(34,760)
Operating Expenses	(11,630)
Interest Expense	(520)
Income Tax Expense	(1,665)
Cash Flow from Operating Activities	$ 3,105

method, the large majority of businesses use the indirect method in their external financial reports (which the FASB permits). Because of its popularity, we use the indirect method for the statement of cash flows in our business example.

Profit Before the Bottom Line

The standard definition of net income, aka bottom line profit, is revenue and income minus *all* expenses and losses. This all-inclusive concept of profit is the foundation of the income statement. In analyzing profit performance, you could exclude certain expenses and not deduct them against revenue and income; of course, this yields a different measure of profit.

One particular such practice has become popular for analyzing profit and cash flow. Profit, or rather we should say earnings, is set equal to net income before interest, tax, depreciation, and amortization (EBITDA). These expenses are set aside and are not deducted against sales revenue and other income. These expenses are added back to net income to get an alternative metric of profit, or *earnings*, as it is called.

For our business example, EBITDA is determined as follows (dollar amounts in thousands from income statement):

Our example does not record an amortization expense, so there isn't one included here.

Net Income	$2,642
+ Interest Expense	$ 545
+ Income Tax Expense	$1,748
+ Depreciation Expense	$ 785
= EBITDA	$5,720

EBITDA can be used as an alternative basis for interpreting operating profit, one that strips away how the company is financed and taxed and removes depreciation and amortization (if the business records any amortization expense). As explained in Chapter 10, determining the amount of annual depreciation to record is arbitrary and typically is not totally consistent with economic reality. How useful EBITDA is as a tool for analysis is open to debate. It may open the door to some useful insights about a business, or it may not. In any case, you see references to EBITDA quite often.

Some analysts argue that EBITDA is a handy shortcut to estimate cash flow from operating activities. However, interest and income tax are certainly cash flow expenses, although they are omitted. When using EBITDA, you should have a crystal-clear understanding that this alternative earnings measure is *not* equal to cash flow from operating activities. As we just said, cash flows for interest and income tax expenses are not taken into account, and other factors affecting cash flow may be ignored as well.

Changes in accounts receivable, inventory, prepaid expenses, accounts payable, accrued expenses payable, and income tax payable are ignored by EBITDA. If all these changes in operating assets and liabilities are relatively minor, then simply adding back depreciation (and amortization, if any) to net income might be acceptable as a cash flow approximation. But typically these changes are significant and should not be ignored.

A final warning: In some financial reports cash flow is pushed to the forefront and profit is pushed to the background. When a business's profit performance is lackluster or when a business reports a loss, the CEO may prefer to shift attention to cash flow (assuming cash flow is healthy). However, cash flow is not a substitute for profit. The oldest trick in the book is diverting attention from bad news to whatever good news you can find. Simply put, profit generates cash flow; cash flow does not generate profit.

Accounting Issues

Most financial statement readers have a good intuitive understanding of a balance sheet (assets, liabilities, and shareholders' equity), and they have a good intuitive understanding that profit equals sales revenue minus expenses. In contrast, most financial statement readers seem confused about cash flow from profit. They think that making profit means making money, and that cash increases the same amount as bottom-line profit. This is not true. Profit and cash flow are two different numbers, both of which are important in their own right.

We remind you that accountants are accrual-basis people, not cash-basis people. To most accountants accrual basis is second nature. Indeed, we've met accountants who have trouble understanding cash flow because they are so submerged in the accrual basis. As a matter of fact, we've seen CPAs who have trouble preparing a statement of cash flows.

In preparing financial reports, accountants should keep in mind that readers generally have a more difficult time understanding the statement of cash flows (particularly the first section) as compared with the balance sheet and income statement. But we see little evidence of this in the actual reporting of cash flow statements. We have read countless statements of cash flows and found that many are exceedingly complicated. It's not unusual to find a statement of cash flows of a public company that reports 30, 40, or more lines of information. Furthermore, it is impossible to reconcile all the items reported in the statement of cash flows with their corresponding assets and liabilities in the balance sheet.

Businesses should provide a readable statement of cash flows. It would be quite helpful if management provided a brief summary and discussion of the company's cash flows for the year. Instead, the large majority of businesses offer little or no comment regarding their cash flows, making it difficult to interpret them. Even CPAs would have trouble doing a complete and thorough analysis of the cash flows statements of many companies.

15

CASH FLOWS FROM INVESTING AND FINANCING ACTIVITIES

Completing the Statement of Cash Flows

Please refer to Exhibit 15.1. The preceding chapter explains the first of the three sections in the statement of cash flows. This chapter explains that statement's other two sections, which are a piece of cake to understand compared with the first section that reports cash flow from operating activities (see Chapter 14).

EXHIBIT 15.1—CASH FLOWS FROM INVESTING AND FINANCING ACTIVITIES

Dollar Amounts in Thousands

BALANCE SHEET	Start of Year	End of Year	Change		STATEMENT OF CASH FLOWS FOR YEAR		
Assets					Net Income—See Income Statement	$ 2,642	
Cash	$ 3,735	$ 3,265	$ (470)		Accounts Receivable Increase	(320)	
Accounts Receivable	4,680	5,000	320		Inventory Increase	(935)	
Inventory	7,515	8,450	935		Prepaid Expenses Increase	(275)	
Prepaid Expenses	685	960	275		Depreciation Expense	785	
Property, Plant, and Equipment	13,450	16,500	3,050		Accounts Payable Increase	645	
Accumulated Depreciation	(3,465)	(4,250)	(785)		Accrued Expenses Payable Increase	480	
Intangible Assets	5,000	5,575	575		Income Tax Payable Increase	83	
Total Assets	**$31,600**	**$35,500**			**Cash Flow from Operating Activities**		**$3,105**
Liabilities and Stockholders' Equity					Investments in Property, Plant, and Equipment	$(3,050)	
Accounts Payable	$ 2,675	$ 3,320	645		Investments in Intangible Assets	(575)	
Accrued Expenses Payable	1,035	1,515	480		**Cash Flow from Investing Activities**		(3,625)
Income Tax Payable	82	165	83				
Short-Term Notes Payable	3,000	3,125	125		Increase in Short-Term Notes Payable	$ 125	
Long-Term Notes Payable	3,750	4,250	500		Increase in Long-Term Notes Payable	500	
Capital Stock	7,950	8,125	175		Issue of Additional Capital Stock Shares	175	
Retained Earnings	13,108	15,000	1,892		Cash Dividends Paid Shareholders	(750)	
Total Liabilities and Stockholders' Equity	**$31,600**	**$35,500**			**Cash Flow from Financing Activities**		50
					Decrease in Cash During Year		$ (470)

The second section of the statement of cash flows (Exhibit 15.1) summarizes the *investment activities* of the business during the year in long-term operating assets. In the example, the business spent $3,050,000 for new fixed assets (tangible long-term operating assets). See the line extending from this expenditure in the statement of cash flows to the property, plant, and equipment asset account in the balance sheet. In addition, the business increased its investment in intangible assets $575,000 during the year.

The investing activities section includes proceeds from disposals of investments (net of tax), if there are any such disposals during the period. In our example, the business did not dispose of any of its long-term operating assets, tangible or intangible, during the year. We should mention in passing that an ongoing business normally makes some disposals of fixed assets during the year.

The third section of the statement of cash flows (see Exhibit 15.1 again) reports the cash flows of *financing activities*. The term *financing* refers to dealings between the business and its sources of capital (i.e., its lenders and its stockholders). The business in our example increased its short-term and long-term debt during the year. It also raised a relatively small amount of $175,000 from issuing new capital stock shares (to key officers of the business).

See the lines of connection from the statement of cash flows to the corresponding balance sheet accounts in Exhibit 15.1.

The business distributed $750,000 in cash dividends from profit to its shareowners during the year. Cash dividends are included in the financing activities section of the cash flows statement. You may logically ask: why not put cash dividends next to cash flow from profit (i.e., from operating activities)? We say more about the placement of cash dividends later in the chapter. Its $2,642,000 net income for the year increases the company's retained earnings account, and the $750,000 cash dividends decrease this shareholders' equity account. Therefore, the net increase in retained earnings during the year is $1,892,000 (see Exhibit 15.1 to check this).

The bottom line of the statement of cash flows is the $470,000 decrease in cash during the year (see Exhibit 15.1). Well, perhaps we shouldn't call the change in cash the *bottom line*. The term *bottom line* is more or less reserved for the last line of the income statement, but we see nothing wrong with using it here to refer to the bottom line of the cash flows statement. That line is the final, net result of all three types of activities that determine the increase or decrease in cash during the year.

Seeing the Big Picture of Cash Flows

Earning profit is a vital source of cash inflow to every business. Profit is the *internal* source of cash flow—money generated by the business itself without going outside the company to secure external sources of capital. Chapter 14 explains that the company generated $3,105,000 cash flow during the year just ended from its operating activities. Profit provided more than $3 million for the business—and that isn't chicken feed.

The obvious question is: what did the business do with its cash flow from profit? The remainder of the cash flows statement answers this important question. The rest of the cash flows statement reports other sources of cash that were tapped by the business during the year that provided additional capital to the business. And, most important, the statement of cash flows reveals what the business did with this money.

From its profit-making activities the company generated $3,105,000 cash during the year. What *could* it do with this money? One option is simply to increase its cash balance—just let the money pile up in the company's checking account. This is not a productive use of the cash, unless the business is on the ragged edge and desperately needs to increase its day-to-day working cash balance. The business could also pay down some of its liabilities. Or, the company could use some of the money to pay cash dividends to its stockholders.

In fact, the business did pay $750,000 in cash dividends to its stockholders during the year. The amount of cash dividends to shareholders is one of the key items reported in the statement of cash flows—see the third section of the cash flows statement in Exhibit 15.1. After subtracting $750,000 cash dividends from the $3,105,000 cash flow from profit, the company had $2,355,000 cash flow remaining from operating activities. You may ask: what did the business do with this cash?

To modernize and expand its production and sales capacity, during the year the business invested $3,625,000 in new long-term operating assets including tangible and intangible assets. These cash outlays are called *capital expenditures*, a term that emphasizes the long-term nature of investing capital in these assets. You may have noticed that the total amount of capital expenditures was considerably more than cash flow from profit net of cash dividends ($3,625,000 capital expenditures less $2,355,000 cash flow from profit net of cash dividends equals $1,270,000 shortfall). This money had to come from somewhere.

A business has three sources to cover such a cash shortfall: (1) borrow more money on short-term and long-term debt, (2) secure additional capital from shareowners by issuing new capital stock shares, and (3) spend down its cash balance. The business in our example did some of all three, as seen in the following summary (amounts from Exhibit 15.1):

Cash Sources Used to Provide Amount Spent on Capital Expenditures During Year in Excess of Cash Flow from Operating Activities Net of Cash Dividends

Increase of Short-Term Debt	$ 125,000
Increase of Long-Term Debt	$ 500,000
Issue of Additional Capital Stock Shares	$ 175,000
Decrease in Cash Balance	$ 470,000
Total	$1,270,000

When a business is growing year to year, its cash flow from profit net of cash dividends typically does not provide all the cash it needs for its capital expenditures. Therefore, the business has to expand its debt and equity capital, which it did in our example.

Business managers, lenders, and investors keep a close watch on capital expenditures. These cash outlays are a bet on the future by the company. The business is saying, in effect, that it needs the new fixed assets to maintain or improve its competitive position, or to expand its facilities for future growth. These are some of the most critical decisions business managers make.

Making capital investments is always risky. On one hand, who knows what will happen in the future? On the other hand, not making such investments may sign the death warrant of a business. By not making such investments, the company may fall behind its competition and lose market share that would be impossible to regain. Then again, being overinvested and having excess capacity can be an albatross around the neck of a business.

In any case, the business laid out $3,625,000 during the year for new assets (see Exhibit 15.1 again). In doing so, the business had to make key financing decisions—where to get the money for the asset purchases. As already mentioned, the business decided it could allow its working cash balance to drop $470,000. The company's ending cash balance is $3,265,000, which, relative to its $52,000,000 annual sales revenue, equals about three weeks of sales revenue.

We should point out that there are no general standards or guidelines regarding how large a company's working cash balance should be. Most business managers would view the company's cash balance in this example as adequate, we think. Just how much cash cushion does a business need as a safety reserve to protect against unfavorable developments? Opinions differ on this question.

What if the economy takes a nosedive, or what if the company has a serious falloff in sales? What if some of its accounts receivable are not collected on time? What if the company is not able to sell its inventory soon enough to keep the cash flow cycle in motion? What if it doesn't have enough money to pay its employees on time? There are no easy answers to these cash dilemmas.

The business could have forgone cash dividends in order to keep its working cash balance at a higher level. In all likelihood, its stockholders want a cash dividend on their investments in the business. The board of directors might have been under pressure to deliver cash dividends. In any case, the business distributed $750,000 cash dividends, which are reported in the financing activities section in the cash flows statement (Exhibit 15.1).

In summary, the cash flows statement deserves as much attention and scrutiny as the income statement and balance sheet. Though not too likely, a company making a profit could be headed for liquidity problems (having too little ready cash) or solvency problems (not being able to pay liabilities on time). Making profit does not guarantee liquidity and solvency. The cash flows statement should be read carefully to see if there are any danger signs or red flags.

At the end of Chapter 14 we mention that statements of cash flows reported by most public corporations are cluttered with a lot of detail—often far too much detail, in our opinion. Our advice is to focus mainly on the big-ticket items and skip the smaller details in reading a statement of cash flows. Stand back and try to see the big picture. The income statements reported by most public corporations have far fewer lines of information compared with cash flows statements and are generally much easier to understand. This is an odd state of affairs indeed.

Accounting Issues

There are several technical accounting problems in reporting cash flows. For example, should the cash flows connected with the discontinued operations of a business be reported separately from its ongoing, recurring cash flows? Should cash flows of certain short-term activities be reported gross or net? These cash flow issues are beyond the scope of this book. (We can almost hear you breathing easier here.)

One thing comes across loud and clear in the authoritative pronouncement on reporting cash flows. A business should not include cash flow per share in its financial reports. In particular, a business should not report cash flow from operating activities per share. Public companies are required to report earnings (net income) per share (EPS). The accounting authorities do not want financial statement readers to confuse EPS with cash flow.

One of our criticisms of the statement of cash flows—aside from the huge number of lines reported by most companies—is the placement of cash dividends in the financing activities section. Instead, we favor placing cash dividends immediately under cash flow from operating activities. Deducting from operating activities the amount of cash dividends that result from cash flow would highlight the amount of cash flow the company had available for general business purposes.

The purpose is to show more clearly how much of the cash flow from profit was available to the business after cash dividends. The financial statement reader could easily size up dividends against the amount of cash flow from profit, and see the amount of cash remaining for other needs of the business. But the current standard is to put dividends in the financing activities section of the cash flows statement. Our view is that businesses should have more options regarding where to place cash dividends in their statements of cash flows.

Part Three

USING FINANCIAL STATEMENTS

16

FOOTNOTES AND MANAGEMENT DISCUSSIONS

This and the following two chapters expand our discussion on analyzing the information presented in financial reports in addition to the three primary financial statements. This chapter explores two basic types of additional information presented in business financial reports, footnotes and management discussions of operating results. *Footnotes* apply to specific metrics and data points to supplement the financial statements included in a financial report. *Management discussions of operating results* is a written assessment of the information presented in the financial statement. In the next chapter (Chapter 17) we explain commonly used *financial statement ratios* and what they mean. In Chapter 18 we explore an important topic that flies under the banner of *financial engineering*.

Financial Report Content in Addition to Financial Statements

When reading this chapter, it is important to keep in mind that while a company's financial statements represent the backbone for analyzing and evaluating its financial performance, financial reports include extensive additional financial, business, legal, and regulatory material that accompany the financial statements. The actual financial statements may occupy anywhere from three to six pages of an external business financial report. But the complete financial report may often exceed 100 pages (compliments of management providing their discussion/assessment of operating results along with the required footnotes that accompany audited financial statements). So, with this said, our discussion starts with the difference between management-provided discussions and financial statement footnotes.

Management Discussion of Operating Results (MDOR): The MDOR or sometimes referred to as the MD&A (i.e., management discussion and analysis) is a section of a business's financial report that is generally reserved for management to provide an assessment or overview of key operating results, market trends, industry data, strategies, and other topics that management believes would be beneficial to external parties to help them more fully understand the operating results of a business. The MDOR is usually located at the front of the periodically prepared, externally distributed financial report and quite often starts with a shareholder or investor letter from the company's chairman of the board, CEO, or other top executive. There is no doubt that the MDOR can provide useful information to external parties, but it should be noted that, generally speaking, the information provided in the MDOR has not been audited by the independent CPA firm. Rather, it contains information that is being presented by a company's management team. Translation: the MDOR tends to include a broader range of business information that has been internally prepared by the company and incorporates more opinions and perspectives than audited financial statements (which tends to stay factual in nature).

Financial Statement Footnotes: Unlike MDOR disclosures, financial statement footnotes are part of the audited financial statements, prepared by an independent CPA firm (with support from company financial executives and legal counsel), and are most often located toward the back of the externally prepared financial report, just after the financial statements. The goal of financial statement footnotes is to provide additional clarity, support, and detail to validate and substantiate the information provided in the financial statements. For example, if a company has established a reserve for a potential liability due to uncertain legal actions brought against the company, the footnote will help shed additional light on the nature of the legal action and potential damages. Generally speaking, financial statement footnotes tend to avoid presenting management opinions and are instead more focused on sticking to the facts, yet even here we must again point out an irony in the accounting and financial reporting world. That is, while the purpose of audited financial statements and associated footnotes is to present external financial reports prepared by independent third-party CPAs that are factual in nature, almost all audited financial statements and associated footnotes rely heavily on the use of estimates when calculating operating results. This concept underscores the importance of remembering that accounting is often just as much an art form as a science!

This chapter and the next, which is on financial statement ratios, refer to information as presented in *external* financial reports, which are those that circulate outside the business. These financial reports and communications are designed mainly for use by external readers, including shareowners, analysts, company lenders, and the like, with the business's shareowners and lenders representing the two primary *stakeholders* in the business.

Internal audiences, including business executives, managers, and staff members, have access to significantly more information than is released in the company's external financial reports. This information tends to be very detailed in nature and is usually highly confidential, so external disclosure is tightly guarded. Diving into a more thorough discussion on internal business information is beyond the scope of this book but it should be noted that, in the words of Warren Buffett, "the devil is in the detail" when analyzing financial information, so it goes without saying that invaluable internal financial information is both highly sought after and closely guarded given its importance.

The balance of this chapter focuses on financial statement footnotes. Attempting to dive into a more detailed discussion and review of the MDOR represents a book unto itself. But again, it is important to understand that almost all externally prepared financial reports include a lengthy, informative, and somewhat subjective section that allows the management team to provide valuable financial and operating business information that all external readers should find useful.

In short, footnotes are the fifth essential part of every CPA-prepared or audited financial report. (The other four are the big three financial statements including the balance sheet, the income statement, and the statement of cash flows, plus, of course, the all-important audit opinion, which is usually located at the front of the audited financial statements.) Financial statements would be naked without their footnotes. This chapter explains the importance of reading the footnotes and the common challenges and problems they can pose. Studying a financial report should definitely include reading the footnotes to the financial statements.

Financial Statements—Brief Review

Before discussing footnotes, let's quickly review the three financial statements of a business that we explain in previous chapters.

1. **Balance sheet:** Also called the *statement of financial condition*, the balance sheet is a relatively brief and condensed summary of a company's assets, liabilities, and owners' (stockholders') equity at the close of business on the last day of the income statement period. In reading a balance sheet, you need to understand the differences between basic types of assets (inventory versus property, plant, and equipment, for instance), and the differences between operating liabilities (mainly accounts payable and accrued expenses payable) versus debt on which the business pays interest. Also, you should know the difference between the two different sources of owners' equity: 1) capital invested by the owners in the business and 2) profit earned and not distributed to owners, which is called *retained earnings*. Finally, a balance sheet can help an external party understand if a company has adequate liquidity to operate (has current assets sufficient to fulfill current liabilities) and whether or not the company is actually solvent (has greater assets than liabilities), two extremely important concepts and discussed further in Chapter 17, which is on ratios.

2. **Income statement:** This financial statement summarizes a company's sales revenue and expenses for the period (the profit-making activities of the business), and it reports the company's bottom-line *net income or net loss* for the period, also referred to as *earnings* and more popularly simply *profit or loss*. A publicly owned business corporation must report its earnings per share (EPS) with its income statement. A nonpublic company doesn't have to report earnings per share but is often provided for informational purposes.

3. **Statement of cash flows:** Making a profit has cash flow effects. But, as discussed in Chapters 3 and 4, the amount of cash flow from making profit during the year does not equal bottom-line profit (net income) for the year. This financial statement divides cash flows into three groups. The first section provides a trail from net income or loss to cash flow from *operating (profit-making) activities*. The second section summarizes the cash flow of the company's *investing activities* during the year. The third section summarizes the cash flow from the company's *financing activities* during the year. The statement of cash flows exposes the financial strategy of the business. For example, you can compare dividends paid during the year against its cash flow from operating activities (profit), which is a major financial decision of the business.

In short, the three financial statements report on the three financial imperatives facing every business—generating a profit (or managing a loss), maintaining a healthy financial condition, and properly managing cash and capital resources.

Most businesses—large and small, public and private—present comparative financial statements for their most recent two to three years of operating results. This multiyear presentation allows financial statement readers to make comparisons between the year just ended and the preceding year, and the year before that. The federal agency that regulates financial reporting by public corporations, the Securities and Exchange Commission (SEC), requires three-year comparative financial statements.

According to various estimates, there are approximately 3,600 *public* companies in the United States (estimated as of 2017), a number that has decreased from over 7,000 roughly two decades ago. There are several reasons for the decrease including public companies going private, mergers and acquisitions reducing the number of companies, and the fact that operating as a public company is both very expensive and involves additional risks. The financial statements and footnotes of the financial reports of public companies are required to be audited annually by an independent certified public accountant (CPA) firm. The largest four international CPA firms (called the *Big Four*) audit the large majority of public companies. There are millions of *private* businesses in the United States. Private companies may or may not have their financial reports audited by an independent CPA firm. Generally, they are not legally required to have audits. (We discuss financial report audits and reviews in Chapter 19.)

Why Footnotes?

Without footnotes, financial statements would be incomplete, and possibly misleading. Footnotes are an essential *extension* to the three primary financial statements. Each financial statement is presented on one or, at most, two pages in a financial report. Keep in mind that each financial statement is very condensed and presents highly compacted information.

It comes down to this: the lenders and investors in a business, as well as external analysts, need more information than can be put into the financial statements. We suppose you could integrate this additional information into each financial statement. But can you imagine reading a balance sheet or an income statement that runs 5, 10, or 20 pages? We don't think so. Therefore, the practical solution is to present the additional information in the form of supplementary footnotes to the financial statements. If you have a financial stake in the business, you definitely should read the footnotes to its financial statements.

One overarching premise of financial reporting is *adequate disclosure*, so that all those who have a legitimate concern about the financial affairs of the business are provided the relevant information they need to make informed decisions and to protect their interests. Footnotes are needed because they provide additional information that is important to financial statement readers.

Top-level managers should not forget that they are responsible for the company's financial statements *and the accompanying footnotes*. The footnotes are an integral, inseparable part of a financial report. Financial statements state this fact on the bottom of each page, usually worded as follows:

The accompanying footnotes to the financial statements are an integral part of these statements.

The CPA auditor's report includes an audit opinion and covers footnotes, as well as the financial statements.

Ideally, footnotes should be written in an understandable manner, and every effort should be made to use language and visual layouts, schedules, and exhibits that are clear and reasonably easy to follow. In other words, financial reports should be *transparent*. The lack of transparency in financial reports has come in for much criticism, especially regarding footnotes that are so dense and obtuse that even a lawyer would have trouble reading them. More on this point later in the chapter.

Two Types of Footnotes

One type of footnote identifies and discusses the key accounting methods used by the business. For several types of expenses and even when recognizing sales revenue, a business can choose between two (or more) acceptable accounting methods. Needless to say, the company's selection of accounting methods should be made clear in its footnotes and should generally be applied in a consistent manner. When a company elects to change accounting methods, your ears should definitely perk up, leading you to wonder why now, for what reason, and so on.

A footnote is needed for each significant accounting choice elected by the business. Here's an example of the types of accounting methods footnotes you find in financial reports (at least in the reports of public companies). In a recent financial report the company included footnotes explaining its accounting methods for the following items:

- Nature of operations (construction products versus financial products)
- Basis of presentation (consolidation methods)
- Sales and revenue recognition (a detailed list)
- Inventories (use of the LIFO method and effects if the alternative FIFO method had been used)
- Depreciation and amortization
- Foreign currency translations

- Derivative financial instruments
- Income taxes
- Estimates in financial statements
- New accounting guidelines (standards) that took effect in the year
- Goodwill
- Accumulated other comprehensive income
- Assets held for sale
- Equity incentive plans and stock-based compensation

Often footnotes occupy more pages than the financial statements themselves, which is generally the rule rather than the exception.

Warning: Footnotes assume that you are familiar with general accounting terminology. A business may be in an industry that is relatively unique and very different than most other businesses, in which case it might explain unusual terminology in its footnotes. But, by and large, companies do not include a glossary of accounting terms to help readers of their financial reports.

Most large businesses consist of a family of corporations under the control of one parent company. The financial statements of each corporation are grouped together into one integrated set of financial statements. Intercorporate dealings are eliminated as if there were only one entity. Affiliated companies in which the business has made investments are not consolidated if the company does not have a controlling interest in the other business.

In addition to footnotes that identify accounting methods, footnotes are needed to provide essential information that cannot be placed in the financial statements themselves. For example, the maturity dates, interest rates, collateral or other security provisions, and other details of the long-term debt of a business are presented in footnotes. In addition, annual rentals and obligations required under short-term and long-term operating leases are also provided. Details regarding stock options and stock-based compensation plans are spelled out as well, and the dilution effects on earnings per share are illustrated in footnotes.

As previously noted, a significant legal action or lawsuit against the company would typically be discussed and disclosed in footnotes. Additionally, details about the company's employees' retirement and pension plans are disclosed in footnotes, as are obligations of the business to pay for postretirement health and medical costs of retired employees.

The list of possible footnote material is long and the final report should include those that encompass all material, significant, and/or impactful events or transactions affecting a business's operations and financial statements. When preparing its annual report, a business needs to go down an exhaustive checklist of items that may have to be disclosed, and then actually write the footnotes. This is no easy task as the business has to explain, in a relatively small space, what can be a rather complex subject matter.

Management Discretion in Writing Footnotes

Business executives have to rely on the experts—the chief financial officer of the organization, legal counsel, and the outside CPA auditor—to go through the checklist of footnotes that may be required. Once every required footnote has been identified, key decisions still have to be made regarding each footnote. A business has a good deal of discretion and latitude regarding just how candid to be and how much detail to reveal in each footnote, but it should be remembered that footnotes are considered part of the audited financial statements and are subject to significant input and approval from the external CPA firm.

Clearly, business managers do not want to give away too much detail or confidential information, as they should not divulge anything that would sacrifice a competitive advantage the business enjoys. It goes without saying that business executives and managers aren't in the business of helping their competition. Rather, the idea is to find the right balance between disclosing the appropriate amount of information to assist the company's creditors, stockholders, and analysts with their evaluations of the business, and reporting all the information such stakeholders are entitled to.

But just how much information do the creditors and stockholders really need? How much are they legally entitled to? These are difficult questions to answer in straightforward and clear-cut terms. Beyond certain basic facts, exactly what should be put in a footnote to comply with the standard of adequate disclosure is not always clear and definite.

Too little disclosure, such as withholding information about a major lawsuit against the business, would be misleading, and the top executives of the business would be liable for such lack of disclosure. Beyond the legal minimum, which should be insisted on by the company's CPA auditors, footnote disclosure rules and guidelines are somewhat vague and murky.

Business executives, in fact, have rather broad freedom of choice regarding how frank to be and how to express what they put in footnotes. Quite clearly, footnotes are not written like newspaper articles. If the company's advertising copy were written like its footnotes, the business wouldn't make many sales.

Analysis Issues

Admittedly, we may be somewhat biased regarding footnotes to financial statements. Excuse us if we jump on the soapbox here. We see a very serious financial reporting problem regarding the readability of footnotes. As authors, we may be overly sensitive to this, but we think not. Investors and securities analysts complain about the dense fog in footnotes. Footnote writing can be so obtuse that you have to suspect that the writing is deliberately obscure. The rules require footnotes, but the rules fail to demand that the footnotes be clear and concise so that an average financial report reader can understand them. As we previously noted, and which is worth mentioning again, accounting is often more of an art than a science. This definitely holds true when preparing footnotes given the importance of the information being disclosed balanced against business confidentiality and clarity of presentation.

All too often the sentence structure of footnotes seems intentionally legalistic and awkward. Technical terminology abounds in footnotes. Poor writing seems more prevalent in footnotes on sensitive matters, such as lawsuits or ventures that the business abandoned with heavy losses. A lack of candor is obvious in many footnotes.

Creditors, analysts, and stockholders cannot expect managers to expose all the dirty linen of the business in footnotes, or to confess all their bad decisions. But, improved clarity and more frankness certainly would help and should not damage the business.

In short, creditors, analysts, and investors often are stymied by poorly written footnotes. You have only one option, and that is to plow through the underbrush of troublesome footnotes, more than once if necessary. Usually you can tell if particular footnotes are important enough to deserve this extra effort. Beyond this advice, all we can say to you regarding reading footnotes is, "Good luck."

17

FINANCIAL STATEMENT RATIOS AND ANALYSIS

Financial Reporting Ground Rules

The main purpose of external financial reporting is to provide up-to-date, complete, accurate, reliable, and timely financial information from a business to shareholders, investors, lenders, analysts, and the like. Investors and lenders are critical external parties as they represent potential sources of capital (debt and equity) and as such, have a right to and need for the information. Other parties are also interested in the financial affairs of a business—for example, its employees, other creditors, analysts (who provide independent assessments of a business), regulatory groups, and so on. When they read financial reports, they should keep in mind that these communications are primarily directed to the owner-investors of the business and its lenders. External financial reporting standards have been developed with this primary audience in mind.

According to estimates, there are about 3,600 publicly owned businesses in the United States. Their capital stock shares and other securities are traded in public markets. The dissemination of financial information by these companies is governed by federal law, which is enforced mainly by the Securities and Exchange Commission (SEC). The New York Stock Exchange, Nasdaq, and Internet securities markets also enforce rules and regulations over the communication of financial information by companies whose securities are traded on their markets.

Securities of foreign businesses are traded in stock markets around the world. Many countries, including the United States, have been attempting to develop a set of *international financial reporting and accounting standards*. This process has not gone as smoothly as many had hoped. Indeed, as of the time of this book's publication, the SEC has not yet given its formal endorsement of international standards. U.S. businesses are not yet required to adopt the global standards.

In the United States and other countries, public companies cannot legally release information to some stockholders or lenders but not to others, nor can a business tip off some of them before informing the others. The laws and established standards of financial reporting are designed to ensure that all stockholders, analysts, and lenders have equal access to a company's financial information and financial reports.

A company's financial report may not be the first source of information about its profit performance. In the United States, most public corporations issue press releases of their most recent earnings results, but it is important to remember that the releases of the earnings may not have been audited by an independent CPA firm. These press releases precede the mailing of hard copies of the company's financial report to its stockholders, lenders, and other parties. Most public companies put their financial reports on their websites at the time of or soon after the press releases. Private businesses do not usually send out letters to their owners and lenders in advance of their financial reports, although they could. As a rule, private companies do not put their financial reports on publicly accessible websites.

This chapter examines what stockholders, lenders, and analysts do with financial reports once they have access to them. The chapter centers on the *annual* financial report. (Quarterly financial reports are abbreviated versions of the annual reports.) In particular, this chapter focuses on financial *statement ratios* that are widely used by investors, lenders, and analysts to evaluate the company's performance and help formulate an opinion on its overall operations.

Financial Statement Preliminaries

Exhibit 17.1 presents a company's annual financial statements. This is the same company example used throughout earlier chapters. The footnotes for these statements are not included. (Chapter 16 discusses footnotes to financial statements.)

EXHIBIT 17.1—EXTERNAL FINANCIAL STATEMENTS OF BUSINESS (WITHOUT FOOTNOTES)

Dollar Amounts in Thousands Except Earnings per Share

INCOME STATEMENT FOR YEAR

Sales Revenue	$ 52,000
Cost of Goods Sold Expense	33,800
Gross Margin	$ 18,200
Selling, General, and	
Administrative Expenses	12,480
Depreciation Expense	785
Earnings Before Interest and Tax	$ 4,935
Interest Expense	545
Earnings Before Tax	$ 4,390
Income Tax Expense	1,748
Net Income	$ 2,642
Basic Earnings per Share	$ 3.30

STATEMENT OF CHANGES IN STOCKHOLDERS' EQUITY FOR YEAR

	Capital Stock	Retained Earnings
Beginning Balances	$ 7,950	$13,108
Net Income for Year		2,642
Shares Issued During Year	$ 175	
Dividends Paid During Year		$ (750)
Ending Balances	$ 8,125	$15,000

BALANCE SHEET AT END OF YEAR

Assets

Cash		$ 3,265
Accounts Receivable		5,000
Inventory		8,450
Prepaid Expenses		960
Current Assets		$ 17,675
Property, Plant, & Equipment	$16,500	
Accumulated Depreciation	(4,250)	12,250
Intangible Assets		5,575
Total Assets		$ 35,500

Liabilities & Owners' Equity

Accounts Payable		$ 3,320
Accrued Expenses Payable		1,515
Income Tax Payable		165
Short-Term Notes Payable		3,125
Current Liabilities		$ 8,125
Long-Term Notes Payable		4,250
Total Liabilities		$ 12,375
Capital Stock (800,000 shares)	$ 8,125	
Retained Earnings	15,000	
Stockholders' Equity		$ 23,125
Total Liabilities & Stockholders' Equity		$ 35,500

STATEMENT OF CASH FLOWS FOR YEAR

Net Income	$ 2,642
Accounts Receivable Increase	(320)
Inventory Increase	(935)
Prepaid Expenses Increase	(275)
Depreciation Expense	785
Accounts Payable Increase	645
Accrued Expenses Payable Increase	480
Income Tax Payable Increase	83
Cash Flow from Operating Activities	**$ 3,105**
Expenditures for Property, Plant, and Equipment	$(3,050)
Expenditures for Intangible Assets	(575)
Cash Flow from Investing Activities	(3,625)
Increase in Short-Term Notes Payable	$ 125
Increase in Long-Term Notes Payable	500
Issue of 7,000 Capital Stock Shares	175
Cash Dividends Paid Shareholders	(750)
Cash Flow from Financing Activities	50
Decrease in Cash During Year	$ (470)
Cash Balance at Start of Year	3,735
Cash Balance at End of Year	3,265

Our company example is privately owned. Its common stock ownership shares are not traded in a public market. The business has about 50 shareholders; some are managers of the business, including the CEO, the president, and several vice presidents. A business this size could go into the public marketplace for equity capital through an initial public offering (IPO) of capital stock shares and become publicly owned. However, the company has decided to remain private.

This chapter does not pretend to cover the field of *securities analysis* (i.e., the analysis of stocks and debt instruments issued by corporations). This broad field includes the analysis of competitive advantages and disadvantages of a business, domestic and international economic developments, business combination possibilities, general economic conditions, and much more. The key ratios explained in this chapter are basic building blocks in securities analysis.

Also, this chapter does not discuss *trend analysis*, which involves comparing a company's latest financial statements with its previous years' statements to identify important year-to-year changes. For example, investors and lenders are very interested in the sales growth or decline of a business, and the resulting impact on profit performance, cash flow, and financial condition.

This chapter has a more modest objective: to explain basic ratios used in financial statement analysis and what the ratios indicate about a business. Only a handful of ratios are discussed in the chapter, but they are fundamentally important and represent those most widely used by industry professionals.

On opening a company's financial report, probably one of the first things most investors do is give the financial statements a once-over; they do a fairly quick scan of them. What do most financial report readers first look for? In our experience, they look first at the bottom line of the income statement, to see if the business made a profit or suffered a loss for the year.

As one sports celebrity put it when explaining how he keeps tabs on his various business investments, he looks first to see if the bottom line has "parentheses around it." The business in our example does not; it made a profit. Its income statement reports that the business earned $2,642,000 net income (i.e., bottom-line profit) for the year. Is this profit performance good, mediocre, or poor? Ratios help answer this question.

After reading the income statement, most financial statement readers probably take a quick look at the company's assets and compare them with the liabilities of the business. Are the assets adequate to the demands of the company's liabilities? Ratios help answer this question.

Extraordinary Gains and Losses

The business in our example does not report any *extraordinary gains or losses* for the year, which are one-time, nonrecurring events. For example, a business may sell a major fixed asset and record a gain. Or a business may record a restructuring charge for the cost of laying off employees who will receive severance packages. These out-of-the-ordinary, unusual gains and losses are reported separately from the ongoing, continuing operations of a company.

Be warned: these irregular gains and losses complicate the evaluation and forecasting of profit performance! Extraordinary gains and losses, especially losses, raise troublesome questions, such as:

- Is an extraordinary loss really a correction of past years' accounting mistakes?

- What if a company reports such irregular gains and losses on a recurring basis (instead of infrequently)?

- Will such extraordinary gains and losses be reported again in the future, and if so, when and how much?

Deciding how to interpret and assess extraordinary gains and losses is a vexing challenge, to say the least.

A New Financial Statement

Exhibit 17.1 introduces a new financial statement—the *statement of changes in stockholders' equity for year*—that we have not presented before in the book. In some respects, this is not really a financial statement; it's more of a supporting schedule that summarizes changes in the stockholders' equity accounts. The business issued 7,000 additional shares of capital stock during the year. The $175,000 cash from issuing the shares are reported in the statement of changes in stockholders' equity as well as the statement of cash flows (see Exhibit 17.1). Net income for the year is reported as an increase in retained earnings, and cash dividends paid to stockholders are a decrease.

The statement of changes in stockholders' equity is definitely needed when a business has a capitalization (ownership) structure that includes two or more classes of stock, and when a business owns some of its own capital stock shares (called *treasury stock*). This financial statement is also needed when a business has recorded certain types of losses and gains that bypass the income statement. The amounts of any such special gains and losses are recorded in a special stockholders' equity account called *Accumulated Other Comprehensive Income*.

The term *comprehensive income* connotes that, in addition to net income that flows through the income statement into the retained earnings account, additional gains and losses have been recorded that have not been reported in the income statement. The accumulated other comprehensive income account serves like a second retained-earnings–type account, which holds the cumulative result of recording certain types of gains and losses. Exploring these special gains and losses would take us into a technical territory beyond the scope of this book.

The statement of changes in stockholders' equity can be complex and highly technical. In the following discussion we focus on the most widely used ratios that are calculated from data in the three major financial statements (i.e., balance sheet, income statement, and statement of cash flows).

Benchmark Financial Ratios

Stock analysts, investment managers, individual investors, investment bankers, economists, and many others are interested in the fundamental financial aspects of a business. Ratios are a big help in analyzing the financial situation and performance of a business. So far in the book only two financial statement ratios have been mentioned: the *accounts receivable turnover ratio* in Chapter 5 and the *inventory turnover ratio* in Chapter 6. At this point you might be anticipating that we will begin with profit analysis. No, we start with *solvency*.

Solvency refers to the ability of a business to pay its liabilities when they come due. If a business is insolvent and cannot pay its liabilities on time its very continuance is at stake. In many respects solvency comes first and profit second (as the first rule in business is to never run out of cash to operate). The ability to earn profit rests on the ability of the business to continue on course and avoid being shut down or interfered with by its lenders. In short, earning profit demands that a business remains solvent. Maintaining solvency (its debt-paying ability) is essential for every business. If a business defaults on its debt obligations, it becomes vulnerable to legal proceedings that could stop the company in its tracks, or at least could interfere with its normal operations.

Bankers and other lenders, when deciding whether to make and renew loans to a business, direct their attention to certain key financial statement ratios to help them evaluate the solvency situation and prospects of the business. These ratios provide a useful financial profile of the business in assessing its creditworthiness and for judging the ability of the business to pay interest and to repay the principal of its loans on time and in full.

Note: For the rest of this chapter, all amounts from the financial statements are in thousands of dollars, except earnings per share (EPS). Instead of reminding you every time, we assume that you remember that the data is taken from Exhibit 17.1.

Current Ratio

The *current ratio* tests the ability of a business to pay its short-term liabilities. It is calculated by dividing total current assets by total current liabilities, using the figures from a company's most recent balance sheet. The current ratio for our example company is computed as follows:

$$\frac{\$17,675 \text{ Current Assets}}{\$8,125 \text{ Current Liabilities}} = 2.18 \text{ Current Ratio}$$

The current ratio is hardly ever expressed as a percent (which would be 218 percent for this company example). The current ratio for the business is stated as 2.18 to 1.00, or more simply just as 2.18.

The common opinion is that the current ratio for a business should be 2 to 1 or higher (although this depends on the type of industry the company operates within as in some instances, current ratios closer to 1.25 to 1.00 are acceptable). Most businesses find that their creditors expect this minimum current ratio. In other words, short-term creditors generally like to see a business limit its current liabilities to one-half or less of its current assets.

Why do short-term creditors put this limit on a business? The main reason is to provide a safety cushion of protection for the payment of the company's short-term liabilities. A current ratio of 2 to 1 means there is $2 of cash and assets that should be converted into cash during the near future that will be available to pay each $1 of current liabilities that come due in roughly the same time period. Each dollar of short-term liabilities is backed up with $2 of cash on hand or near-term cash inflows. The extra dollar of current assets provides a margin of safety for the creditors.

A company may be able to pay its liabilities on time with a current ratio less than 2 to 1, or perhaps even if its current ratio were as low as 1 to 1. In our business example, the company has borrowed $3,125,000 on the basis of short-term notes payable, which equals 18 percent of its total current assets. Its short-term lenders may not be willing to lend the business much more—although perhaps the business could persuade its lenders to go up to, say, $4 million or $5 million on short-term notes payable.

In summary, short-term sources of credit generally demand that a company's current assets be double its current liabilities (again, depending on the industry). After all, creditors are not owners—they don't share in the profit earned by the business. The income on their loans is limited to the interest they charge (and collect). As creditors, they quite properly minimize their loan risks; as limited-income (fixed-income) investors, they are not compensated to take on much risk.

Acid Test Ratio (Quick Ratio)

Inventory is many weeks or months away from conversion into cash. Products are typically held two, three, or four months before being sold. If sales are made on credit, which is normal when one business sells to another business (also called a B-to-B business model), there is a second waiting period before the receivables are collected. In short, inventory is not nearly as liquid as accounts receivable; it takes much longer to convert inventory first into sales and then into cash. Furthermore, there's no guarantee that all the products in inventory will be sold because items can become obsolete, spoiled, lost, stolen, and so on.

A more severe measure of the short-term liability-paying ability of a business is the *acid test ratio* (also called the *quick ratio*), which excludes inventory and prepaid expenses. Only cash, short-term marketable securities investments (if any), and accounts receivable are counted as sources to pay the current liabilities of the business.

This ratio is also called the *quick ratio* because only cash and assets that can be quickly converted into cash are included in the amount available for paying current liabilities. It's more in the nature of a liquidity ratio that focuses on how much cash and near-cash assets a business possesses to pay all of its short-term liabilities.

In this example, the company's acid test ratio is calculated as follows (the business has no investments in marketable securities):

$$\frac{\$3,265 \text{ Cash} + \$5,000 \text{ Accounts Receivable}}{\$8,125 \text{ Current Liablities}} = 1.02 \text{ Acid Test Ratio}$$

The general rule is that a company's acid test ratio should be 1 to 1 or better, although you find many exceptions.

Debt-to-Equity Ratio

Some debt is generally good, but too much debt is dangerous. The *debt-to-equity ratio* is an indicator of whether a company is using debt prudently, or perhaps has gone too far and is overburdened with debt that may cause problems. For this example, the company's debt-to-equity ratio calculation is:

$$\frac{\$12,375 \text{ Total Liabilities}}{\$23,123 \text{ Total Stockholders' Equity}} = 0.54 \text{ Debt-to-Equity Ratio}$$

This ratio tells us that the company is using $0.54 of liabilities in addition to each $1 of stockholders' equity in the business. Notice that all liabilities (noninterest bearing as well as interest bearing, and both short term and long term) are included in this ratio, and that all owners' equity (i.e., invested capital stock and retained earnings) is included.

This business—with its 0.54 debt to equity ratio—would be viewed as moderately leveraged. *Leverage* refers to using the equity capital base to raise additional capital from nonowner sources. In other words, the business is using $1.54 of total capital for every $1 of equity capital. The business has $1.54 of assets working for it for every dollar of equity capital in the business.

Historically, most businesses have tended to stay below a 1-to-1 debt-to-equity ratio. They don't want to take on too much debt or they cannot convince lenders to put up more than one-half of their assets. However, some capital-intensive (asset-heavy) businesses such as public utilities and financial institutions operate with debt-to-equity ratios much higher than 1 to 1. In other words, they are highly leveraged.

But we offer a word of caution in today's world. Over the decade since the Great Recession of 2007 through 2009, the world has been flooded with massive cash infusions from global central banks while undertaking highly accommodative monetary policies and driving interest rates down. By some estimates, over $15 trillion of cash/currency has been injected into the global economy by the world's leading central banks. This has resulted in a drastic decline in interest rates that, unbelievable as it may sound, has resulted in over $15 trillion of global debt generating negative interest rates (yes, you heard us right).

These policy changes have encouraged businesses to secure new and very cheap debt to be used for business purposes ranging from investing in capital equipment to repurchasing its issued shares, helping drive up EPS (refer to Chapter 13) This so-called *easy* monetary environment has unfortunately also produced two unwanted side effects:

1. First, historical "norms" (for lack of a better term) of debt-to-equity ratios of, let's say, less than 1 to 1 (as previously noted) have been sacrificed in the name of cheap (i.e., low interest rates), abundant (i.e., large amounts of fresh/new capital), and easy (i.e., limited financial performance covenant requirements) debt. So not only are companies becoming more and more leveraged, the quality of the debt, via establishing performance covenants to ensure a company's performance is acceptable, is being reduced or in some cases eliminated. It doesn't take a genius to quickly conclude that a more-leveraged company with lower-quality debt is generally a recipe for disaster.

2. Second, when companies use debt to repurchase their own shares (a very common practice over the past three years), the number of shares outstanding when calculating its EPS decreases (e.g., Company XYZ had 1 million shares outstanding and elected to repurchase 100,000 leaving 900,000 shares remaining as outstanding). With fewer outstanding

shares and a relatively constant net profit, the company provides the appearance, or some may say illusion, that its EPS is increasing even though its net profit did not change. This concept is a perfect example of what is commonly referred to as *financial engineering*, a topic that we will dig into in Chapter 18. It is something that is extremely important to understand in today's global economy.

Times-Interest-Earned Ratio

To pay interest on its debt, a business needs to have sufficient earnings before interest and income tax, a metric referred to as EBIT. The *times-interest-earned ratio* is calculated to test the ability to pay interest from earnings. Annual earnings before interest and income tax is divided by interest expense:

$$\frac{\$4,935 \text{ EBIT}}{\$545 \text{ Interest Expenses}} = 9.1 \text{ Times-Interest-Earned Ratio}$$

There is no standard or general rule for this particular ratio—although obviously the ratio needs to be higher than 1.00 to 1.00 and really should be well north of 2.00 to 1.00 (see the debt service coverage ratio that follows). In this example, the company's EBIT is more than nine times its annual interest expense, which is comforting to its lenders. Lenders would be alarmed if a business barely covered its annual interest expense. (The company's management and stockholders should be equally alarmed.)

Return-on-Sales Ratio

Making sales while controlling expenses is how a business makes profit. The profit residual slice from a company's total sales revenue pie is expressed by the *return-on-sales ratio*, which is profit divided by sales revenue for the period. The company's return on sales ratio for its latest year is:

$$\frac{\$2,642 \text{ Net Income}}{\$52,000 \text{ Sales Revenue}} = 5.1\% \text{ Return-on-Sales Ratio}$$

There is another way of explaining the return-on-sales ratio. For each $100 of sales revenue, the business earned $5.10 net income—and had expenses of $94.90. Return on sales varies quite markedly from one industry to another. Some businesses do well with only a 2 percent return on sales; others need more than 10 percent to justify the large amount of capital invested in their assets.

Return on Equity (ROE)

Owners take the risk of whether their business can earn a profit and sustain its profit performance over the years. How much would you pay for a business that consistently suffers a loss? The value of the owners' investment depends first and foremost on the past and potential future profit performance of the business—or not just profit, we should say, but profit relative to the capital invested to earn that profit.

For instance, suppose a business earns $100,000 annual net income for its stockholders. If its stockholders' equity is $250,000, then its profit performance relative to the stockholders' capital used to make that profit is 40 percent, which is very good indeed. If, however, stockholders' equity is $2,500,000, then the company's profit performance equals only 4 percent of owners' equity, which is weak relative to the owners' capital used to earn that profit.

In short, profit should be compared with the amount of capital invested to earn that profit. Profit for a period divided by the amount of capital invested to earn that profit is generally called *return on investment* (ROI). ROI is a broad concept that applies to almost any sort of investment of capital.

The owners' historical investment in a business is the total of the owners' equity accounts in the company's balance sheet. Their profit is bottom-line net income for the period—well, maybe not all of net income. A business corporation may issue *preferred stock* on which a fixed amount of dividends has to be paid each year. The preferred stock shares have the first claim on dividends from net income. Therefore, preferred stock dividends are subtracted from net income to determine the *net income available for the common stockholders*. In this example the business has issued only one class of stock shares. The company has no preferred stock, so all of net income belongs to its common stockholders.

Dividing annual net income by stockholders' equity gives the *return-on-equity* (ROE) ratio. The calculation for the company's ROE in this example is:

$$\frac{\$2,642 \text{ Net Income}}{\$23,125 \text{ Stockholders' Equity}} = \frac{11.4\% \text{ Return-on-}}{\text{Equity Ratio}}$$

Note: We use the ending balance of stockholders' equity to simplify the calculation. Alternatively, the weighted average during the year could be used—and should be if there have been significant changes during the year.

By most standards, this company's 11.4 percent annual ROE would be acceptable but not impressive. However, everything is relative. ROE should be compared with industry-wide averages and with investment alternatives. Also, the risk factor is important. Just how risky is the stockholders' capital investment in the business?

We need to know much more about the history and prospects of the business to reach a final conclusion regarding whether its 11.4 percent ROE is good, mediocre, or poor. Also, we should consider the *opportunity cost of capital*—that is, the ROI the stockholders could have earned on the next-best use of their capital. Furthermore, we have not considered the personal income tax on dividends paid to its individual stockholders. In summary, judging ROE is not a simple matter!

Return on Assets (ROA)

Here's another useful profit performance ratio:

$$\frac{\$4,935 \text{ EBIT}}{\$35,500 \text{ Total Assets}} = \frac{13.9\% \text{ Return-on-}}{\text{Assets Ratio}}$$

The *return-on-assets* (ROA) ratio reveals that the business earned \$13.90 before interest and income tax expenses on each \$100 of assets. The ROA is compared with the annual interest rate on the company's borrowed money. In this example, the company's annual interest rate on its short-term and long-term debt is 7.5 percent. The business earned 13.9 percent on the money borrowed, as measured by the ROA. The difference or spread between the two rates is a favorable spread equal to 6.4 percentage points, which increases the earnings after interest for stockholders. This source of profit enhancement is called *financial leverage gain*. In contrast, if a company's ROA is less than its interest rate, it suffers a financial leverage loss.

Earnings per Share (EPS)

In contrast to the ratios discussed earlier in the chapter, the earnings-per-share (EPS) ratio is reported at the bottom of their income statements by public companies. You don't have to calculate it. Given its importance, you should surely understand how it is calculated. Private companies are not required to report EPS but many larger, more sophisticated private companies do report this figure. As a stockholder of a private company, you may find it helpful to calculate EPS.

The capital stock shares of 3,600 domestic business corporations are traded in public markets—the New York Stock Exchange, Nasdaq, and electronic stock exchanges. The day-to-day, even minute-by-minute market price changes of these shares receive a great deal of attention. More than any other single factor, the market value of capital stock shares depends on the past and forecast net income (earnings) of a business.

Suppose we tell you that the market price of a stock is $60, and ask you whether this value is too high or too low, or just about right. You could compare the market price with the stockholders' equity per share reported in the balance sheet—called the *book value per share*, which is about $29 in our example. (Recall that a company's total assets minus its total liabilities equal its stockholders' equity.) The book value method has a respectable history in securities analysis. Today, however, the book value approach plays second fiddle to the earnings-based approach. The starting point is to calculate *earnings (net income) per share*.

EPS is one of the most widely used ratios in investment analysis. The essential calculation of earnings per share for our company example is as follows:

$$\frac{\$2{,}642 \text{ Net Income Available for Common Stockholders}}{800{,}000 \text{ Shares of Common Stock Outstanding}} = \frac{\$3.30 \text{ Basic Earnings}}{\text{per Share}}$$

Note: To be technically accurate, the weighted average number of shares outstanding during the year should be used—based on the actual number of shares outstanding each month (or day) during the period.

First off, notice that the numerator (top number) in the EPS ratio is *net income available for common stockholders*, which equals bottom-line net income less any dividends paid to the preferred stockholders of the business. As mentioned earlier, many corporations issue preferred stock that requires a fixed amount of dividends to be paid each year. The mandatory annual dividends to the preferred stockholders are deducted from net income to determine net income available for the common stockholders.

Second, please notice the word *basic* in front of *earnings per share*, which means that the actual number of common stock shares in the hands of stockholders is the denominator (bottom number) in the EPS calculation. Many business corporations have entered into contracts of one sort or another that require the company at some time in the future to issue additional stock shares at prices below the market value of the stock shares at that time. The shares under these contracts have not been actually issued yet but probably will be in the future.

For example, business corporations award managers *stock options* to buy common stock shares of the company at fixed prices (generally equal to the present market price or current value of the shares). If, in the future, the market value of the shares rises over the fixed option prices, the managers will exercise their rights and buy capital stock shares at a bargain price. With stock options, therefore, the number of stock shares is subject to inflation. When (and if) the additional shares are issued, EPS will suffer because net income will have to be spread over a larger number of stock shares. EPS will be diluted, or thinned down, because of the larger denominator in the EPS ratio.

Basic EPS does not recognize the additional shares that will be issued when stock options are exercised. Also, basic EPS does not take into account potential dilution effects of any convertible bonds and convertible preferred stock that have been issued by a business.

These securities can be converted at the option of the security holders into common stock shares at predetermined prices.

To warn investors of the potential effects of stock options and convertible securities, a second EPS is reported by public corporations, called fully *diluted* EPS. This lower EPS takes into account the potential dilution effects caused by issuing additional common-stock shares under stock-option plans, convertible securities, and any other commitments a business has entered into that could require it to issue additional stock shares at predetermined prices in the future.

Basic EPS and fully diluted EPS (if applicable) must be reported in the income statements of publicly owned business corporations. This indicates the importance of EPS. In contrast, none of the other ratios discussed in this chapter have to be reported, although many public companies report selected ratios.

Price/Earnings (P/E) Ratio

The market price of stock shares of a public business corporation is compared with its EPS and expressed in the *price/earnings (P/E) ratio* as follows:

$$\frac{\text{Current Market Price of Stock Shares}}{\text{Earnings per Share}} = \text{Price/Earnings Ratio}$$

Suppose a public company's stock shares are trading at $40 per share and its basic EPS for the most recent year (called the *trailing 12 months*) is $2. The company does not report a diluted EPS. Thus, its P/E ratio is 20. Like other ratios discussed in this chapter, the P/E ratio should be compared with industry-wide and market-wide averages to judge whether it is acceptable, too high, or too low. At one time, a P/E ratio of 8 was considered right. As we write this sentence, P/E ratios in the range of 15 to 18 are considered acceptable and nothing to be alarmed about.

Now, here's a problem in calculating the P/E ratio for a public company: Should you use its *basic* EPS or its fully *diluted* EPS? If the business reports only basic EPS, there is no problem. But when a public company reports both, which EPS should you use? Well, it is done both ways. Our advice is to check the legend in the stock market tables in the *Wall Street Journal* and *The New York Times* to find out which EPS the newspaper uses in reporting the P/E ratios for companies. Using diluted EPS is more conservative; that is, it gives a higher P/E ratio.

The market prices for stock shares of private businesses are not available to the public at large. Private company shares are usually not actively traded, and when they are traded, the price per share is not made public. Nevertheless, stockholders in these businesses are interested in what their shares are worth. To estimate the value of stock shares a P/E multiple can be used. In the company example, its EPS is $3.30 for the most recent year (see Exhibit 18.1). Suppose you own some of the capital stock shares, and someone offers to buy your shares. You could establish an offer price at, say, 12 times basic EPS. This would be $39.60 per share. The potential buyer may not be willing to pay this price, or he or she might be willing to pay 15 or 18 times basic EPS.

Market Cap

Suppose the stock shares of a public company are currently trading at $65 per share, and the business has 10 million shares outstanding. The *market cap*, or total market value capitalization of the company, is $650 million ($65 market value per share × 10 million capital stock shares = $650 million). We'd bet you dollars to doughnuts that if you compared the market cap of most businesses with the shareholders' equity amounts reported in their latest balance sheets, the market caps would be considerably higher— perhaps *much* higher.

The book value (balance sheet value) of shareholders' equity is the historical record of the amounts invested in the business by the owners' past plus its retained earnings accumulated over the years. Over time, these amounts become more and more out of date. In contrast, the market cap is based on the current market value of the company's stock shares. If a business gets into financial straits, its market cap may drop below the book value of its owners' equity—at least for the time being. In rare cases a company's cash balance may be more than its market cap.

Two Cash Flow Ratios to Chew On

The ratios that have been associated and analyzed so far have tended to focus on the income statement and balance sheet (ignoring the cash flows statement). This is traditionally where most parties focus their attention because the information gleaned from the calculations is very useful. But cash flow ratios and analyses are just as informative and, in today's world, have become mainstays when evaluating a company's operating performance and financial viability. Here, we present two cash-flow–based ratios and analysis tools that are widely used in the market:

1. **Debt-Service-Coverage Ratio (DSCR)**: Expanding on the times-interest-earned ratio, we now turn to the DSCR ratio. This ratio starts with the same EBIT figure but now divides it by the annual interest expense, plus the debt principal payments due over the next year. The goal with this expanded ratio is to ensure that the company not only has the ability to cover its interest expense but also, make all necessary debt principal payments as well. Using the above information, we will add $1,700 of principal debt service payments due over the next 12 months. The $1,700 figure is based on the assumption that the long-term debt balance of $4,250 is due and payable over approximately the next 2.5 years (which could be confirmed with the debt payments in the cash flow statement or if forward looking, in the company's footnotes, as discussed in Chapter 16). Here's our calculation:

$4,935 EBIT/$2,245 ($545 Interest Expense plus $1,700 of debt principal payments) = 2.20 Debt-Service-Coverage Ratio

Again, it goes without saying, this ratio needs to be north of 1.00 to 1.00, with most lenders demanding a minimum ratio of at least 1.25 to 1.00 (and often higher). So, the good news for our example company is that their 2.20 DSCR is well above these targets but it does highlight the importance of managing available cash flow in relation to both total interest expense and debt principal payments due.

2. **Adjusted EBITDA**: To recap, EBITDA stands for earnings before interest, taxes, depreciation, and amortization expense. Typically, it is not separately disclosed in a company's financial report, so it must be calculated. Adjusted EBITDA is calculated by increasing EBITDA for expenses or charges that are considered non-recurring or one-time in nature and then decreasing EBITDA for normal and customary capital expenditures that must be incurred to ensure continued operating performance levels. For example, a manufacturing company must constantly invest in new equipment to support business operations (as the old equipment becomes obsolete and/or is worn-out through depreciation). In our sample company, adjusted EBITDA would be calculated as follows:

$4,935 of EBIT plus $785 of depreciation equals $5,720 of EBITDA.

Assuming no expense addbacks, this figure would then be reduced by $3,050 of capital expenditures (from the cash flow statement) producing adjusted EBITDA of $2,670.

So far this doesn't look so bad, but when evaluating this against total debt service requirements of $2,245 (see above), dividends paid of $750 (from the cash flow statement) and income tax expense of $1,748, the company actually came up short on the cash front by $2,073 (i.e., a negative internal cash flow calculated by taking $2,670 less $2,245 of debt service less $750 of dividends less $1,748 of income tax expense). It is no wonder that the company had to raise cash from issuing new debt and equity during the year to help finance its operations.

So, the real question with this calculation is: does this indicate a problem? For the year, the company didn't generate enough internal cash flow to cover all expenses, support required capital expenditures, and meet total debt service during the year. This, of course, could be an anomaly for the current year (as capital expenditures were elevated and most likely will decrease the next year) or it could highlight a deeper problem with cash and capital management leading to the need to eliminate dividends, restructure long-term debt (to be paid over a longer period), and so on. In any case, this result warrants a deeper dive into the company's financial reports and its plans to gain additional clarity on any potential issues or problems that might be coming down the road.

Final Comments

Many other ratios can be calculated from the data in financial statements. For example, the *asset turnover ratio* (annual sales revenue divided by total assets) and the *dividend yield* (annual cash dividends per share divided by market value per share) are two ratios you often see used in securities analysis. There's no end to the ratios that can be calculated.

The trick is to focus on those ratios that have the most interpretive value. It's not easy to figure out which ratios are the most important. Professional investors seem to use too many ratios rather than too few, in our opinion. However, you never know which ratio might provide a valuable clue to the future direction of a stock's market value.

18

FINANCIAL ENGINEERING

What Financial Engineering Is Not

Before we dive into the concept of financial engineering and what it entails, it's helpful to identify what financial engineering is not. We want to put out of your mind any preconceived notions about the topics of fraudulent financial reporting or heavy-handed manipulation of accounting and other deliberately misleading information put into financial reports.

There are two specific points that are important to understand:

1. Financial engineering does not refer to the intentional misreporting and misleading presentation of accounting transactions and financial operating results. It does not refer to cooking the books. While we would love to recall some of the great accounting frauds of the past (e.g., Enron), this subject would warrant a whole book to itself. We just point out here that almost all "great" accounting frauds were supported by executive-level management collusion. Multiple members of the executive management team worked in complicity to report financial information with the willful intent to deceive and mislead. We offer here only a couple of advisory points to remember when it comes to fraudulent financial information. Be on the lookout for any signs of executive-level collusion, such as boards of directors that aren't truly independent. Be careful if the CPA auditor of the financial report is relatively unknown. Finally, be extra careful of tightly controlled insider-operated businesses, which are more conducive to accounting and financial reporting abuse.

2. Financial engineering usually does not refer to companies adopting aggressive accounting methods and highly favorable estimates for recording transactions and reporting financial operating results. Using aggressive accounting methods by itself does not represent a fraudulent activity as long as the accounting methods fall within the guidelines of generally accepted accounting principles (GAAP). The use of one accounting method over another is a decision best left for the company's management team, board of directors, and independent auditors to resolve and agree upon. With this said, we would offer a tip as it relates to sniffing out companies that may be utilizing more aggressive accounting methods than are justified. Aggressive accounting methods can be used to accelerate sales revenue and defer expenses, thereby inflating earnings. While this makes the income statement look good and gives the appearance of strong profits, don't forget that the income statement is generally the easiest of the three fundamental financial statements to manipulate. This is one reason we emphasize the importance of understanding how cash is generated and consumed in a business, which can readily be found in the cash flows statement.

What Financial Engineering Is

So now that we know what financial engineering is not, let's explore what financial engineering refers to. First, we encounter a problem. The term has more than one meaning. Broadly speaking, it refers to the use of highly sophisticated mathematical methods and computer-based algorithms for analyzing financial reports data. Here we use the term *financial engineering* in an important but much more limited sense.

In the rest of the chapter, we use the term to refer to going a step beyond simple ratios to use other techniques for analyzing and reconfiguring financial report information. This additional layer of analysis may very well sway or shift the reader's sentiment about a company's operating performance and financial position. The primary goal of financial engineering, as we use the term in this chapter, is to assist external parties with gaining a better understanding of a business's reported operating results and financial position. One example of how businesses themselves do financial engineering directly in their financial reports concerns the issue of *extraordinary gains and losses*.

Companies have been able to produce financial statements that present core operating results and carve out extreme or unique, one-time events that negatively impacted net profits (called extraordinary events) during a specific reporting period. For example, a manufacturing company based in the American South might have experienced a massive, once-in-a-generation loss from a devastating weather event such as a hurricane. With the loss being so significant and the event so unusual, it would not be expected to recur for quite a while, so it could be captured as a one-time loss reported as *other expenses* in the income statement (below the operating income level). By carving out this rather unusual expense, an external reader of the financial statements could clearly and efficiently understand why the company incurred such a large loss, allowing him or her to focus on the remaining base operations to evaluate the company's financial performance.

Up to this point, we're in agreement that presenting more complete, accurate, and revealing financial operating results in the financial statements is warranted and beneficial to outside parties. But it is also at this point where the concept of modern-day financial engineering needs to be appreciated and that accounting as an "art" form versus a science needs to be clearly understood by defining financial engineering in the simplest form.

Financial engineering is based in the idea of taking GAAP financial statements and accounting information (as presented) and then engineering, or rearranging the information into a different format, structure, comparison, and so on. The *engineered* data should offer invaluable additional information and perspectives for the purpose of allowing users to make better-informed business decisions. Without the engineered information, external parties may depend solely on a financial report, which can manipulate or distort information that could lead external parties to different conclusions on a company's financial performance and position.

When undertaking financial engineering, you take GAAP financial information and reconfigure it into a different financial framework. In doing this you will start to notice a series of rather commonly used terms and expressions frequently associated with companies that present financially engineered information. These terms, usually abbreviated with acronyms, include non-GAAP, adjusted GAAP, EBITDA or adjusted EBITDA, proforma results, sales bookings, and free cash flow. The list goes on and on. Your antennae should definitely be raised and you should plan to apply additional scrutiny to the information when this type of terminology appears. Generally speaking, the risk of the information not being in compliance with GAAP increases because consistency may be lacking when it comes to how companies define, interpret, and present this information. Furthermore, companies may be much more selective in the type of information they present (to influence/direct a reader toward a specific conclusion). *In short, financially engineered information, by itself, is not fraudulent in nature but rather a somewhat subjective method of reporting financial results that warrants additional scrutiny from external parties.*

Ultimately, it is up to the financial report reader to decide how important the financially engineered information is, how credible it is, and whether it should be relied upon. There's no real school for this other than knowledge and experience, which we hope to help you build, at least a little bit, with our book and specifically this chapter.

Common Types of Financial Engineering

Now that we've helped provide a little more clarity on what constitutes financial engineering, its time to consider a handful of financial engineering examples that have been used (or) abused, over the past two or more decades. This list is by no means all-inclusive but rather is designed to provide a smattering of the breadth of tools and strategies used by companies to highlight (and we use this term with an abundance of caution) certain operating results.

To start, we offer three examples of financial engineering that are fully blessed by GAAP but need deeper dives to properly understand a company's financial performance:

1. ***Discontinued Operations and/or Extraordinary Events:*** We previously touched on this topic as it relates to properly disclosing an extraordinary, one-time event that is material and unusual in nature. We agree with this concept as these types of events are best reported in a clear, concise, and separate manner. Where companies begin to push the limit on this concept and enter into somewhat of a gray zone can be found in two primary areas.

   a. First, are we truly dealing with a one-off event or does the company have a habit of reporting these types of losses year after year? You would be amazed at how many companies convince themselves that a bad business decision warrants a separate disclosure in the financial statements as an extraordinary event (ensuing that the loss was beyond the control of management). When a pattern of continued losses from these types of events emerges period after period, you have to ask if it is really a one-off event or just a means to deflect external parties from bad business decisions being made by the company's management team.

   b. Second, the definition of what constitutes an extraordinary event is often very subjective. GAAP and other accounting pronouncements attempt to provide guidance on this subject but, ultimately, the disclosure decision is generally made by the company's executive management team and external auditors. Furthermore, definitions may change over time when operating in different business environments, when new management teams are brought on board, and so on. This leads to consistency concerns over different reporting periods, which makes it difficult to compare performance over time.

2. **Stock Buybacks:** Over the past five years, stock buybacks have been one of the hottest topics in the financial community. On the surface, when a company buys back its own stock the results often look great. This is because when EPS is calculated as profit and divided over fewer outstanding shares, it increases. From a GAAP perspective, this is technically correct because the remaining shareholders have the right to increased earnings moving forward (so EPS would be higher). But digging deeper, you must ask if this type of transaction or event represents real internal growth that is sustainable year over year or whether it has actually weakened the company's financial position by increasing debt levels (thus increasing financial leverage) or reducing cash holdings (and liquidity)?

3. **Tax Rates and Jurisdictions:** In 2018, the Trump Administration spearheaded a meaningful change to the tax code, which included, among other things, a significant decrease to corporate marginal tax rates. Of course, this was hailed by the corporate world as a significant win. By lowering income tax rates, corporate profits would automatically increase, which was generally the case. But again, and similar to the concept of stock buybacks, the question of sustainability needs to be addressed as when external parties compared a company's 2017 net profit (assuming a 35 percent tax rate) against its 2018 net profit (assuming a 21 percent tax rate), the resulting appearance of significant growth in EPS was artificially bumped higher for a one-year period (e.g., whether the company really realized a 22 percent increase in earnings). However, when 2018 and 2019 operating results are compared, the impact of the lower tax rate will have passed, and a more stable picture of real earnings growth emerges. This concept can also be expanded to companies utilizing or leveraging low-tax-rate jurisdictions to massage net income (e.g., sheltering earnings in foreign countries that have very low corporate tax rates). Again, the question has to be asked whether this is a real benefit or simply a company being more interested in playing a shell game with taxable income. The lesson here is simple: It is important to not rely on changing tax laws or profit-shifting strategies (to manage earnings so they appear higher) as a cure-all for what ails a business. (In the end, if a company is losing money, income taxes are really a moot point.) It goes without saying that proper comparisons at equivalent tax rates should be completed.

Next we provide three examples of what we'll call the *real* or *pure* financial engineering strategies that are outside the scope of GAAP but are frequently utilized by companies:

1. **EBITDA and Addbacks:** First we need to ask the question as to why is EBITDA important. Simply put, EBITDA is a measurement of internal cash flow used to: a) evaluate a company's ability to service debt or support distributions/dividends and, b) relied upon as a basis for valuing a business (e.g., when one company is looking to buy another business). It should make sense that a higher EBITDA generally translates into the ability for a company to support higher debt levels. It also indicates the company's value is higher.

Special Note: We need to emphasize that the concept of EBITDA is definitely subjective and for the most part beyond the scope of GAAP (so it needs to be taken with a grain of salt). But where the real fun begins with EBITDA is when companies start to discuss or disclose adjusted EBITDA with operating performance addbacks. "What are addbacks?" you might ask. Are such addbacks really nothing more than management's assessment of either increased revenue (that should have been earned but for some reason wasn't) or decreased expenses (that will be non-recurring) that should be included or added back in calculating adjusted EBITDA to support a valuation analysis, debt service calculation, and so on. At this point, it should be abundantly clear just how badly not only EBITDA, but addbacks can be abused to inflate earnings and company valuations to achieve a financial objective. Countless examples of the aggressive use of addbacks to inflate EBITDA could be provided, but the general concept we're driving home is that adjusting EBITDA is a very common strategy and negotiating point when negotiating a financial transaction that can be manipulated beyond belief.

2. **Sales Revenue Recognition:** One of the hottest and most important topics in GAAP relates to recognizing sales and determining when the earnings process is complete. More than a few accountants and authoritative groups have weighed in on this subject; as with so many types of sales transactions utilized in the global economy today, there is no shortage of opinions and fact patterns available to help guide a company with recognizing sales revenue. Furthermore, there are a number of subjective elements that must be taken into consideration when recognizing sales revenue, ranging from the validity of the sale to begin with (at the initial point of sales) through to the ultimate collectability of the sale (can the customer even pay). What companies have begun to do on a more frequent basis is to present a non-GAAP sales revenue to reflect, for example, just how many bookings they have (but have not yet delivered to the market or have not satisfied the tests to fully realize the sales revenue in the current period). Is this useful information? Absolutely. But does it mean the company has actually earned the revenue/sales? Absolutely not! So take care to understand the difference between GAAP-recognized sales revenue and the countless other forms of non-GAAP sales revenue a company may disclose.

3. **Proforma Operating Results:** Another very common non-GAAP financial disclosure and analysis companies like to provide relates to presenting proforma operating results. For example, a company may undertake a major acquisition toward the end of the year. Suppose the acquisition holds the promise of significant expense reductions being realized over the next two to three years with the combined operations because economies of scale are realized with large personnel expense reductions anticipated. So, a company may take actual, audited GAAP-based financial results for both companies and then present a hypothetical combination of the two entities as if they were operating together and just how many costs/expenses could be eliminated. Again, this information may be very interesting, but is it 100 percent factual and supported by an audit? Generally not, and it may not be in 100 percent compliance with GAAP. One thing is for certain: the information is highly dependent on management assessments and estimates that are based on forward-looking statements that may or may not come to fruition.

Final Word

We conclude our discussion on financial engineering by emphasizing once again that there is nothing inherently illegal or dishonest about providing supplemental information, which is often very useful to external parties. But in the same breath, it is important to note that this type of information tends to be much more subjective in nature, and is provided to sway or influence external-party analysis of a company, often not in conformity with GAAP and generally not audited by an external CPA firm. Red flags should be raised when you see terms like *EBITDA*, *adjusted GAAP*, *proforma*, *non-GAAP*, *booked revenue* (not yet earned), and the list goes on and on. Make sure you pay close attention to the information and understand the source and purpose of why this it is being presented.

19

CPAs AND FINANCIAL REPORTS

So, you are one of the stockholders in the business example we use throughout the book. You have just received a copy of the company's annual financial report. Can you rely on the information in the annual report? Do the company's accounting methods and disclosures abide with generally accepted standards? Having a certified public accountant (CPA) involved in the financial reporting process is a good idea. CPAs are the experts in accounting and financial reporting. You may know that CPAs audit financial reports, but they also provide a variety of financial reporting services as well as income tax and consulting services.

Certified Public Accountant (CPA)

A person needs to do three things to become a CPA. He or she must earn a college degree with a major in accounting with a fairly heavy load of accounting and auditing courses. The American Institute of Certified Public Accountants (AICPA) has encouraged all states to enact laws requiring five years of education. Most but not quite all states have passed such laws.

Second, a person must pass the national CPA exam, which is a rigorous exam testing knowledge in accounting, income tax, auditing, and business law. Third, a person must satisfy the experience requirement of the state in which he or she lives. State laws and regulations differ regarding the time and nature of public accounting experience that a person must have; one year is generally the minimum.

After the three requirements are completed—education, exam, and experience—the person receives a license from his or her state of residence to practice as a CPA. No one else may hold him- or herself out to the public as a CPA. Most states (perhaps all, but we haven't checked this out) require continuing education each year to renew a person's CPA license. Every state has a Board of Accountancy that regulates the practice of public accounting and has the power to revoke or suspend the licenses of individuals who violate the laws, regulations, and ethics governing CPAs.

CPAs do more than just audit financial reports. They offer an ever-widening range of services to the public, including income tax compliance and planning, personal financial consulting, business valuation, computer systems and information technology, production control and efficiency, forensic functions, and other fields of specialization. CPA firms that audit the financial reports of *public* companies are under tight restrictions regarding which particular nonaudit services they can provide to their audit clients. These restrictions are to maintain the independence of the CPA firm.

The CPA license is widely recognized and highly respected as a professional credential. The professional status of CPAs rests on their expertise and experience, and their independence from their clients. The word *certified* in their title refers to their expertise and experience. The term *public* refers to their independence. In doing audits of financial statements, the independence of the CPA is absolutely essential. To be independent, a CPA must be in public practice and not be an employee of any organization (other than the CPA firm itself).

Public accounting experience is a good stepping stone to other career opportunities. Many persons start in public accounting and end up as the controller (chief accountant), financial vice president, or chief financial officer (CFO) of an organization. Some CPAs become presidents and chief executive officers (CEOs) of business organizations. Some CPAs go into politics (a few have become state governors). Persons who have left public accounting are still referred to as CPAs even though they are not in public practice any longer. This is like a person with an MD degree who leaves the practice of medicine but is still called *doctor*.

From Preparation to Audit of Financial Reports by CPAs

A CPA can offer a variety of services to small and larger clients. One thing the CPA can do is to work with the client in preparing its regular financial reports. The CPA functions as a part-time, in-house chief accountant for the client. The CPA is not an employee, but rather, an independent contractor. Over the years, the CPA may get to know the business quite well. The CPA may or may not call the shots in deciding which accounting methods to use and on decisions regarding what to disclose and not to disclose in the company's financial reports.

In providing this *preparation* service (as it is called), the CPA does not have to assess whether or not he or she is independent in preparing the financial reports of the business. Which brings up an important point. CPAs are generally viewed as *independent* (in addition to being competent on accounting and financial reporting matters of course). This premise is the foundation for the public's trust in CPAs. So, when it comes to other financial reporting services, CPAs are held to a high level of independence. The highest level of independence is demanded when CPA does an audit of a financial report, which we get to in just a minute. First, we have to mention other financial services CPAs offer.

A CPA may be hired to assist the client in the preparation of its financial report or other type of financial information without doing any verification of the information being used to prepare the output. This is called a *compilation*. The CPA doesn't challenge or test the information being used by the client. The CPA does not give any assurance regarding the result of the compilation. The CPA must be independent and say so in a report.

Yet another service a CPA may provide is called a *review*. Frankly, this is a technically confusing area. A review is less than a full-fledged audit (discussed next) but much more than a compilation. The CPA, who must be independent of the client, issues a report. Basically, the CPA says whether or not he or she is aware of any modifications that should be made in order for the client's financial report to be in accordance with relevant accounting and financial reporting standards.

One note: All services offered by a CPA are under the purview of the relevant standards established by the American Institute of Certified Public Accountants (AICPA), or the Public Company Accounting Oversight Board (PCAOB).

Why Audits?

A business may hire an independent CPA to audit its financial report. Many people think an audit is done for the purpose of discovering wrongdoing or ferreting out dishonest and illegal behavior. A CPA is duty bound to maintain a mental attitude of professional skepticism in doing an audit. In carrying out audit procedures, the CPA may discover embezzlement or theft by employees, or uncover accounting fraud orchestrated by high-level managers. These are by-products or side effects of an audit. The main purpose of an audit by a CPA is something else.

The CPA auditor examines accounting records and gathers other evidence in order to render an opinion on the financial report of the business. Based on the audit, the CPA attests, or swears to the *fairness* of the financial statements and disclosures in the financial report of the business. Fairness means, primarily, that the company's accounting methods and disclosures are in accordance with established accounting and financial reporting standards that apply to the entity. In short, the CPA auditor states whether or not the business is playing fairly according to the rules in its financial report.

Suppose you have invested a fair amount of money in a privately owned business. You are not involved in managing the company; you're an absentee owner—a passive investor. Being a stockholder, you receive the company's financial reports. You read the financial statements and footnotes to keep informed about how the company is doing, and whether there might be any storm clouds on the horizon.

Let us ask you a question: how do you know whether the company's financial statements provide adequate disclosure and whether the business uses proper accounting methods to measure its profit? Do you just presume this? Are you sure you can trust the company's financial reports?

Or suppose you are a bank loan officer. A business includes its latest financial statements in its loan application package. Does the business use correct accounting methods to prepare its financial statements? Have the financial statements been tweaked for purposes of securing the loan, to make them look better than they really are? It's not unheard of, you know. (And, as we have said before, the business could be massaging the numbers in its financial statements.)

Or suppose you're a mutual fund investment manager in charge of a large portfolio of stocks traded on the New York Stock Exchange and Nasdaq. Market values of stock shares depend on the net income and earnings per share amounts reported by companies in their financial reports. How do you know that their profit numbers are reliable?

Financial statements can be seriously misleading for two basic reasons, one type being innocent in nature, and the other type not so innocent:

1. *Honest mistakes and incompetence:* A company may not have adequate internal accounting controls. Accounting errors can become imbedded in its accounting records, and

the business may fail to detect and correct the errors. Or, its chief accountant may not understand current accounting and financial reporting requirements and standards.

2. **Deliberate dishonesty:** The top-level managers of a business may intentionally distort the company's profit performance and financial statements, or withhold vital information that should be disclosed in the financial report. This is called financial reporting fraud or accounting fraud. More colloquially, it's called *cooking the books.*

One way to protect against the risks of errors and fraud is to conduct an *audit* of the accounting system of the business by an independent expert accountant, to ascertain whether its financial statements are free of errors and adhere to appropriate accounting and financial reporting standards. The audit provides reassurance that the company's financial report is reliable and follows the rules. Audits of financial reports are done by independent CPAs.

Corporations whose debt and stock securities are traded publicly are required by federal securities laws to have their annual financial reports audited by an independent CPA firm. According to a recent survey there are about 3,600 companies listed on major securities exchanges in the United States (which is down considerably from just a few years ago). The number of private businesses, in the usual sense of the word *business*, is more difficult to pin down. In the United States there are more than 9 million for-profit business corporations, partnerships, and limited liability companies, as well as millions of sole proprietorships (one-owner business ventures). Private businesses are not covered by federal securities laws, but are subject to such state laws as apply to them.

Although they are not *legally required* to have audits, many private business entities have their annual financial reports audited by a CPA firm. Lawyers should be consulted regarding state corporation and securities laws; an audit may be required in certain situations. A private business may sign a contract or agree informally to have its annual financial reports audited by an independent CPA as a condition of borrowing money or when issuing capital stock to new investors in the business.

Public corporations have no choice; they are legally required to have audits of their annual financial reports by an independent CPA firm. But, if not required, should a business hire a CPA firm to audit its annual financial report? What's the payoff? Basically, an audit adds *credibility* to the financial report of a business. Audited financial reports have a higher level of credibility than unaudited statements.

Audits by CPAs provide protection against misleading financial statements. CPA auditors are expert accounting detectives, and they thoroughly understand accounting and financial reporting standards. Being independent of a business, the CPA auditor should not tolerate a misleading financial report.

Audits don't come cheap. CPAs are professionals who command high fees. A business cannot ask for an "once-over lightly" audit at a cut rate. An audit is an audit. CPA auditors of private businesses are bound by *generally accepted auditing standards* (GAAS), and the auditors of public companies have to follow the regulations of the federal agency created by the Sarbanes-Oxley Act of 2002. Violations of auditing standards and regulations can result in lawsuits against the CPA, sanctions by the federal regulatory agency, and damage to the CPA's professional reputation.

An audit takes a lot of time because the CPA has to examine a great deal of evidence and make many tests of the accounting records of the business before being able to express an opinion on the company's financial statements. The time it takes to complete an audit causes the relatively high cost of the audit. A business, assuming an audit is not legally required, has to ask whether the gain in credibility of its financial report is worth the cost of the audit.

A bank may insist on an audit as a condition of making a loan to a business. The outside (nonmanagement) stockholders of a business may insist on annual audits to protect their investments in the business. In these situations, the audit fee can be viewed as a cost of using external capital. In many situations, however, outside investors and creditors do not insist on audits. Even so, a business may choose to have an audit as a checkup on its accounting system. Or a business may decide it needs to have a forensic check— an independent examination focusing on whether the business is vulnerable to fraud and embezzlement schemes.

The auditor does not examine every transaction of a business during the year and does not examine every item making up the total balance of specific assets and liabilities. In a word, auditors rely a great deal on *sampling*. CPA auditors, therefore, pay particular attention to the *internal controls* of the company that are designed to deter and detect errors and irregularities. CPA auditors are required to carry out *risk assessment procedures*, to identify the likely areas of errors and irregularities and to concentrate their audit procedures in the high-risk areas.

CPA auditors are required to plan their audit procedures to search for possible accounting fraud and to identify weak internal controls that would allow such fraud to go undetected. Nevertheless, the main purpose of an audit is to express an opinion on the fairness of financial statements (including footnotes), and whether the financial statements adhere to appropriate accounting and financial reporting standards.

Fraud would undermine the integrity of the financial statements, so the CPA auditor has to be on the lookout for fraud of all types (as well as for accounting errors). But the CPA says nothing at all about fraud in the audit report. There is no statement such as, "We looked for fraud but didn't find any."

Do Auditors Discover Financial Reporting Fraud?

In earlier chapters we distinguish between *massaging the numbers* and *accounting fraud*. Massaging the numbers involves nudging accounting numbers one way or the other. Business managers take actions to control the amounts of sales revenue and expenses recorded in the period, in order to smooth profit year to year or to give profit a temporary boost up (or a push down). Such accounting tactics are in a gray area of accounting ethics. CPA auditors certainly don't like to discover these management machinations regarding the accounting numbers. However, manipulating the accounting numbers is tolerated in the business world—as long as it doesn't go too far so as to cause seriously misleading financial statements.

Massaging the numbers can be likened to a misdemeanor. In this vein, accounting fraud is a felony. Cooking the books goes way beyond nudging the numbers up or down a little. Accounting fraud involves falsification or fabrication of sales revenue and expenses. It includes reporting assets that don't exist and omitting liabilities that do exist. In short, accounting fraud creates financial statements that are deliberately misleading—and seriously so.

Do CPA auditors always discover accounting fraud? The short answer is: not necessarily. CPA auditors *may* discover accounting fraud. However, if the managers who commit fraud cleverly conceal their actions and if their schemes are well thought out, accounting fraud can go undiscovered for years. There are many examples of companies carrying on fraud for 5 or 10 years or more. In many cases the fraud collapses under its own weight or there is evidence that the company's financial report was seriously misleading or fraudulent.

someone blows the whistle. But, having an audit by an independent CPA certainly increases the chances of uncovering accounting fraud, even though the audit does not guarantee that fraud will be uncovered in every instance.

What it comes down to, in our view, is that the cost of an audit has to be kept under control. The audit cost has to be reasonable relative to the benefits of the audit. Given the cost constraint on an audit, the CPA cannot search and test for every conceivable fraud that could be going on in the business. The CPA auditor should evaluate the controls established by the business to guard against financial reporting fraud. If the auditor discovers weaknesses in these controls, he or she should investigate the vulnerable areas and work closely with the company's audit committee to remedy the weaknesses.

At the end of the day, there's always some risk that the CPA auditor may not discover accounting fraud—especially if the top-level managers of the business instigate and orchestrate the fraud. The cost of making all audits absolutely fail-safe would be prohibitive. In the grand scheme of things, a few audit failures are tolerated in order to keep the overall cost of audits within reason. In moments of deep cynicism, it has occurred to us that perhaps the real reason for audits is to provide business lenders and investors someone else to sue when they suffer losses and there is evidence that the company's financial report was seriously misleading or fraudulent.

20

BASIC QUESTIONS, BASIC ANSWERS

Some years ago, a women's investment club invited John to their monthly meeting to speak about financial reports. It was a lot of fun. These women were a savvy group of investors who pooled their monthly contributions. They invested mainly in common stocks actively traded on the major securities exchanges. Our comments in this chapter apply to public corporations as well as private businesses.

These women investors asked thoughtful questions, which we share in this chapter, along with a couple of other questions that are important for anyone who invests in stock and debt securities issued by public corporations, or who has an investment in a private business. Other financial statement readers will also find this chapter helpful.

Business investors and lenders should know the answers to certain questions concerning financial statements. We answer these questions from the viewpoint of a typical individual investor, not an institutional investor or a professional investment manager. John's retirement fund (TIAA) manages almost $1.0 trillion in investments. We assume its portfolio managers know the answers to these questions. They'd better!

When You Buy Stock Does the Company Get Your Money?

One point caught John quite by surprise, and it's an important one to understand. At that time, the women were thinking of buying common stock shares of General Electric (GE). Two members presented their research on the company with the recommendation to buy the stock at the going market price. The discussion caused John to suspect that several of the members thought their money would go to GE. John pointed out that the money would go to the seller of the stock shares, not to GE.

They were not entirely clear on the difference between the *primary* capital market (the original issue of securities by corporations for money that flows directly into their coffers), and the *secondary* securities trading market (in which people sell securities they already own to other investors, with no money going to the companies that originally issued the securities). John compared this with the purchase of a new car in which money goes to General Motors, Ford, or Honda (passing through the dealer) versus the purchase of a used car in which the money goes to the previous owner.

John cleared up that point, although he thinks they were disappointed that GE would not get their money. Once John pointed out the distinction between the two capital markets, they realized that, whereas they were of the opinion that the going market value was a good price to buy at, the person on the other side of the trade must think it was a good price to sell at.

Are Financial Reports Reliable?

Yes, the large majority of financial reports by *public* companies are presented fairly according to established standards, which are called *generally accepted accounting principles* (GAAP) in the United States and *international financial reporting standards* (IFRS) outside the United States. If not, the company's CPA auditor calls deviations or shortcomings to your attention. So, be sure to read the CPA auditor's report. The U.S. and international accounting and financial reporting standards have not been completely merged into one set of converged standards.

The financial reports of *private* companies that are audited by CPAs are as generally reliable as those of public companies. (At least this has been our experience.) However, *unaudited* financial reports of private companies are more at risk of violating one or more accounting and financial reporting standards. For example, we have seen private company annual financial reports that did not include a statement of cash flows, even though this financial statement is required. Much depends on the competence of the chief accountant of the business. When reading unaudited financial statements of smaller private companies, you should be more on guard, particularly if there is no statement of cash flows in the annual financial report.

You should realize that accounting and financial reporting standards are not static. The rule-making authorities constantly monitor financial reporting practices and identify emerging problem areas. They make changes when needed, especially to keep abreast of changes in business and financial practices, as well as developments in the broader political, legal, and economic environments in which businesses live and operate.

Are Some Financial Statements Misleading and Fraudulent?

Unfortunately, despite standards and auditing, some financial statements contain information that is misleading or outright false. The *Wall Street Journal* and *The New York Times* carry stories of accounting fraud instigated by high-level managers in businesses. These financial-report shenanigans are done in various ways. Sales revenue can be overstated. Expenses and losses can be understated or not recorded at all. Net income can be inflated in order to prop up the market price of the stock shares. Or, a business may not disclose serious problems in its financial condition. In committing accounting fraud, the business lies to its lenders and shareowners. The company deliberately misleads its stakeholders by reporting false financial information, and the managers know that it is false.

It is difficult for CPA auditors to detect accounting fraud that is instigated and implemented by high-level managers, especially if it is cleverly concealed and involves conspiracy among managers and other parties to the fraud. (Chapter 19 discusses financial statement audits by CPAs.) Auditors are highly skilled professionals, and the failure rate of auditors to discover fraud has been relatively low. However, in some cases CPAs, including those with the Big Four international CPA firms, were negligent in carrying out their audit procedures or they were complicit with management. The CPA firm deserved to be sued—and were!

The bottom line is that there is a small risk that the financial statements you depend on are, in fact, false and seriously misleading. You would have legal recourse against the company's executives and its CPA auditors once the fraud is found out, but this is not a happy situation. Almost certainly you'd end up losing money, even after recovering some of your losses through legal action.

Should You Take the Time to Compute Financial Statement Ratios?

We doubt it. The conventional wisdom is that by diligently reading financial statements you will discover under- or overvalued securities. However, the evidence doesn't support this premise. Market prices reflect all publicly available information about a business, including the information in its latest quarterly and annual financial reports. (Insiders may be privy to information about coming events and take advantage of their position to make trades before the information becomes public knowledge.)

Computing financial statement ratios can be a valuable learning experience. But don't expect to find out something that the market doesn't already know. It's unlikely that you will find a nugget of information that has been overlooked by everyone else. Forget it; it's not worth your time as an investor. The same time would be better spent keeping up with current business and economic developments reported in the financial press.

Why Read Financial Statements, Then, If You Won't Find Information That Has Been Overlooked by Others?

You should know what you are getting into. Does the company have a lot of debt and a heavy interest load to carry? For that matter, is the company in bankruptcy or in a debt workout situation? Has the company had a consistent earnings record over the past 5 to 10 years, or has its profit ridden a roller coaster over this time? Has the company consistently paid cash dividends for many years? Has the company suffered a major loss recently? Has the company given its executives stock options on a large number of shares? Has the company issued more than one class of stock shares?

Before seriously considering buying a house, you would obviously inspect it to see if it is in good condition and whether it has two stories, three or more bedrooms, a basement, a good general appearance, and so on. Likewise, you should know the "financial architecture" of a business before investing your capital in its securities. Financial statements serve this getting-acquainted purpose very well, as long as you know what to look for.

One basic stock investment strategy is to search through financial reports or websites containing financial statement data to identify corporations that meet certain filtering criteria. For example, you may refine your search so you can see only companies with market values less than their book values, or with cash and cash equivalent per share that are more than a certain percentage of their current market value. Whether these stocks end up beating the market is another matter. In any case, financial statements can be culled through to find whatever types of companies you are looking for.

The Financial Statements and Footnotes of Large Public Companies Would Take Several Hours to Read Carefully: What's the Alternative?

Large businesses produce large financial reports! Their financial statements generally are long, complex, and include several pages of densely written footnotes. Quite literally it would take you several hours, or even longer, to conscientiously read every item in all the financial statements of a company, and every sentence in every footnote. Also, don't forget the auditor's report (also written in technical language), the letter from the CEO to shareholders, and the statement by top management concerning its responsibility for internal controls designed to prevent fraudulent financial reporting. We have to wonder whether professional stock analysts and investment managers have the time to read through the complete financial reports of all the companies they follow and invest in. Maybe they delegate this job to their subordinates, in which case we hope *they* have the time and understand financial statements.

Being aware of how long it takes to read their financial reports cover to cover, most public companies provide *condensed annual financial statements* to their shareholders. The actual financial statements of the business are collapsed into brief summaries of their income statement, balance sheet, and statement of cash flows. These condensed financial statements are *not* accompanied by footnotes and often do not refer to the CPA auditor's report.

If you don't have time to delve into the actual financial statements and footnotes of a company, you should at least read its condensed financial statements. This is better than nothing. By the way, most not-for-profit organizations (such as AARP, for example) issue condensed financial statements to their members. In some situations, we still want to read the actual financial statements. As we start reading them we know we're in for a long night that only an accounting professor could love.

Is There a Basic Test to Gauge a Company's Financial Performance?

We suggest that you compute the percent increase (or decrease) in sales revenue this year compared with last year, and use this percent as the baseline for testing changes in bottom-line profit (net income) as well as the changes in the major operating assets of the business. Assume sales revenue increased 10 percent over last year. Did profit increase 10 percent? Did accounts receivable, inventory, and long-term operating assets increase about 10 percent?

This is no more than a so-called quick-and-dirty method, but it does point out major disparities. For instance, suppose inventory jumped 50 percent even though sales revenue increased only 10 percent. This may signal a major management mistake; the overstock of inventory might lead to write-downs later. Management does not usually comment on such disparities in financial reports. You'll have to find them yourself—and hope you do not find many.

Do Financial Statements Report the Truth, the Whole Truth, and Nothing but the Truth?

The masthead of *The New York Times* boasts "All the News That's Fit to Print." Don't expect this in companies' financial reports, however. There are really two questions here. One question concerns how truthful is profit accounting, which depends on the company's choice of accounting methods from the menu of generally accepted alternatives and how faithfully the methods are applied year in and year out. The other question concerns how honest and forthright are the disclosures in the company's financial report.

Revenue and expenses should be recorded honestly and consistently according to the accounting methods adopted by the business. In other words, once accounting choices have been made, the business should apply the methods and let the chips fall where they may. However, there is convincing evidence that managers of public companies occasionally, if not regularly, intervene and take certain actions to affect the amounts recorded in sales revenue and expenses. They do this to produce more favorable results than would otherwise happen—something akin to the "thumb on the scale" trick.

Manipulating the accounting numbers is done to smooth reported earnings, to balance out unwanted perturbations and oscillations in annual earnings. Investors in public companies seem to prefer a nice steady trend of earnings instead of unpredictable fluctuations, and managers oblige. So, be warned that annual earnings are probably smoothed to some extent.

Disclosure in financial reports, both in the footnotes and in other places, leaves a lot to be desired. Both public and private companies are generally reluctant to lay bare all the facts of interest to their lenders and shareholders. Bad news is usually suppressed or at least deemphasized as long as possible. Clearly, there is a lack of candor and frank discussion in many financial reports. Few companies are willing to wash their dirty linen in public by making full disclosure of their mistakes and difficulties in their financial reports. One notable exception to this reluctance to share bad news is the annual letter to the stockholders by Warren Buffett, chairman of Berkshire Hathaway. He lays both good news and bad news on the line, and admits his mistakes.

Public companies include a *management discussion and analysis* (MD&A) section in their annual financial reports. Usually this is a fairly sanitized version of what happened during the year, often focusing on the favorable results and glossing over the unfavorable. The history of financial reporting disclosure practices, unfortunately, makes clear that until standard-setting authorities force specific disclosure standards on companies, few will make such disclosures voluntarily.

Some years ago the disclosure of employee pension and retirement costs went through this pattern of inadequate reporting until, finally, the standard-setting body in the United States stepped in and required fuller disclosure. Recalls of unsafe products, pending lawsuits, and top management compensation are examples of reluctant reporting. Here is a historical example: Until the standard was adopted in 1987, companies did not report a statement of cash flows, even though this information had been asked for by security analysts since the 1950s!

Does Its Financial Report Explain the Basic Profit-Making Strategy or Profit Model of a Business?

Not really. In an ideal world, we would argue, a financial report should not merely report how much profit (net income) was earned by the business and the amounts of revenue and expenses that generated this profit. The financial report should also provide a profit road map, or an earnings blueprint of the business. The financial report should clarify the so-called business model of the company. Financial report readers should be told the basic profit-making strategy of the business, including its most critical profit-making success factors.

In their annual financial reports, publicly owned corporations are required to disclose their sales revenue and operating expenses by major segments (lines of business). Segmenting a business into its major lines of sales provides information about which major product lines are more profitable than others. However, segments are conglomerate totals that span many different products. Segment disclosure was certainly a step in the right direction. For example, the breakdown between domestic versus international sales revenue and operating profit is important for many businesses.

Businesses are careful not to divulge too much information in their financial reports about their profit margins on specific products (and services). For example, Apple does not reveal the gross margin it makes on sales of its iPhone versus its iPad. Profit margin information is treated as confidential, and is kept away from competitors and from investors in the business as well. The income statement in an external financial report is not the profit report you would see if you were the CEO of the business.

Does the Market Price of a Public Company's Stock Shares Depend Directly and Only on the Information Reported in Its Financial Statements?

Well, you know the answer to this question, don't you? The market price of a public company's stock shares depends on many factors, although the information reported in its financial statements is the main point of reference. We include this question only to remind you that a public company's financial statements are only one source—albeit one of the most important sources—of the information that investors use to make their buy, hold, and sell decisions.

Does the Balance Sheet of a Private Business Tell the Market Value of the Business?

No. The balance sheet of a private business does not report what the market value of the company would be if the business as a whole were on the auction block. The dollar amounts you see in a balance sheet are the results of its actual transactions and operations. The net income (bottom-line profit) reported in the annual income statement of a business summarizes its actual sales revenue for the year minus its actual expenses for the period. Likewise, the cash flows reported by the business are the actual amounts of cash flowing through the business during the year. In short, financial statements are prepared on a "look-back" or historical basis, not on a "look-ahead" basis for determining the market value of the business.

Until there is a serious buyer, it's anyone's guess how much a private business is worth. A buyer may be willing to pay much more than the book value of its owners' equity that is reported in its most recent balance sheet. The market value depends on many factors, as you probably know. Even Warren Buffett, the sage investor who is CEO of Berkshire Hathaway, admits that he has made mistakes in amounts he paid for some businesses in his annual letter to stockholders (which you can download from the company's website).

Generally, the market value of a private business depends mainly on its profit-making ability projected into the future. A buyer may be willing to pay 10 times the annual net income of a privately held business. But we would quickly add that other factors could also play a dominant role in setting the market value of a private business.

Also, we should mention that earnings-based values are quite different from liquidation-based values for a business. Suppose a company is in bankruptcy proceedings or in a troubled debt work-out situation. In this unhappy position, the claims of its debt securities and other liabilities dominate the value of its stock shares and owners' equity. Indeed, the company's stock shares may have zero value in such cases.

Do Books on Investing and Personal Finance Refer to Financial Statements?

It may come as a surprise, but generally these books say little to nothing about financial statements. The books make little effort to explain even the basics of financial statements or they ignore the subject altogether. Don't get us wrong. There are many excellent books on investing and personal finance, and we have read quite a few of them.

We feel obligated to warn you that some of the most popular of these books contain little practical advice that you can actually use. Some of these books explain, for example, that if you save 10 percent of your annual income and invest it wisely,

then after 40 years you will have a nice sum of money. As John's grandkids would say, "Duh!" In any case, we are perplexed that so few of the good investing and personal finance books discuss financial statements in any depth, or they ignore financial statements altogether.

Financial statements are the essential wellspring of information for business investors and lenders. Indeed, where else do you get this vital information? Not having this financial information would be like trying to find your destination in a city without street signs and traffic signals.

A Very Short Summary

You can generally rely on financial statements, although the rash of accounting frauds over the past two or three decades that CPA auditors failed to discover shook our confidence somewhat. Overall, the percent of fraudulent financial reports among all public businesses is low (but not zero). In any case, investors don't really have an alternative source of financial information about a business other than its financial statements. Accounting fraud, unfortunately, is an unavoidable risk of investing.

You might think twice before investing much time in analyzing the financial statements of corporations whose securities are publicly traded—because thousands of other investors have done the same analysis, and the chance of your finding out something that no one else has yet discovered is virtually nil. For a quick benchmark test, though, you might compare the percent change in the company's sales revenue over past year with the percent changes in its net income and operating assets. Major disparities are worth a look.

Reading financial statements is the best way to get acquainted with the financial structure of a business that you're thinking of investing in. Don't worry too much about the accounting methods used by public companies. For privately owned companies, however, you should keep an eye on the major accounting policies of the business and how these accounting methods affect reported earnings and asset values.

Disclosure in financial statements leaves a lot to be desired. Don't look for a road map of the profit strategy of a business in its financial reports. Keep in mind that the total value of a business is not to be found in its balance sheet. Until an actual buyer of a business makes a serious offer, there is no particular reason to determine the value of the business as a going concern. Value depends mainly on the past earnings record of the business as forecast into the future.

The main message of this chapter is to be prudent and careful in making decisions based on financial statements. Many investors and managers don't seem to be aware of the limitations of financial statements. Used intelligently, financial reports are the indispensable starting point for making investment and lending decisions. We hope this book helps you make better decisions. Good luck, and be careful out there.

ABOUT THE AUTHORS

John A. Tracy (Boulder, Colorado) is Professor of Accounting, Emeritus, at the University of Colorado at Boulder. Before his 35-year tenure at Boulder, he was on the business faculty for four years at the University of California, Berkeley. Early in his career he was a staff accountant with Ernst & Young. John is the author of several books on accounting and finance, including *Accounting for Dummies, Accounting Workbook for Dummies, The Fast Forward MBA in Finance, Cash Flow for Dummies,* and *Small Business Financial Management Kit for Dummies* with his son Tage C. Tracy. John received his BSC degree from Creighton University. He earned his MBA and PhD degrees at the University of Wisconsin in Madison. He is a CPA (inactive status) in Colorado.

Tage C. Tracy (Anthem, Arizona) has operated a financial consulting firm focused on providing executive-level accounting, financial and risk management, and strategic business planning management support to private businesses, on a fractional basis. Tage specializes in businesses operating at distinct stages, including startups and launches, rapid growth, ramp-up and expansion management, and strategic exit. He also has expertise in acquisition preparedness and management, turn-arounds, challenging environments, and survival techniques.

Tage has now coauthored a total of six books with his father John A. Tracy including *The Comprehensive Guide on How to Read a Financial Report, Cash Flow for Dummies, Small Business Financial Management Kit for Dummies,* and *How to Manage Profit and Cash Flow.*

Tage received his baccalaureate in accounting in 1985 with honors from the University of Colorado at Boulder. Tage began his career with Coopers & Lybrand (now part of PricewaterhouseCoopers) and obtained his CPA certificate in the state of Colorado in 1987 (now inactive). (His first name, pronounced *tog*, is of Scandinavian origin.)

You can find John and Tage online at: http://financemakescents.com/.

INDEX

U

University of California at Berkeley, 34, 179
University of Colorado at Boulder, 179, 180
University of Wisconsin at Madison, 179
Unpaid expenses, 7, 19, 56, 58, 59, 63, 78, 79, 82; *see also* Liabilities

W

Wall Street Journal, 141, 167
Warranty and guarantee costs, 79
Work-in-process inventory, 46,
Write down (write off) of assets, 15, 48, 75, 76, 102, 171